Enhancing Self-Esteem in the Classroom

Dr **Denis Lawrence** is a chartered educational psychologist and qualified teacher with experience in primary and secondary schools as well as university departments and colleges of education. He is now in private practice as a counsellor and educational consultant. This book is based on research he has carried out over the last three decades both in Australia and in the United Kingdom.

Enhancing Self-Esteem in the Classroom

Third edition

DENIS LAWRENCE

P·C·P
Paul Chapman
Publishing

First edition published 1988
Second edition published 1996
This third edition published 2006

 Paul Chapman Publishing
A SAGE Publications Company
1 Oliver's Yard
55 City Road
London EC1Y 1SP

SAGE Publications Inc
2455 Teller Road
Thousand Oaks, California 91320

SAGE Publications India Pvt Ltd
B-42, Panchsheel Enclave
Post Box 4109
New Delhi 110 017

Library of Congress Control Number: 2005934897

A catalogue record for this book is available from the British
Library

ISBN 10 1-4129-2110-4   ISBN 13 978-1-4129-2110-7
ISBN 10 1-4129-2111-2   ISBN 13 978-1-4129-2111-4 (pbk)

Typeset by Dorwyn Ltd, Wells, Somerset
Printed in Great Britain by T.J. International, Padstow,
Cornwall

Printed on paper from sustainable resources

*For my grandchildren, Sophie, Eve, Patrick, Lula and Lochie
whose joyful enthusiasm continually serves to enhance my own
self-esteem*

Learning begins in pleasure and thrives on curiosity.
(Baughman, 1919)

Through the enhancement of self-esteem we can achieve this goal
and also ensure effective learning.

Contents

Acknowledgements

There would not be sufficient space to acknowledge all those people who have been influential in my writing of this book. Room must be found, however, for some.

I remain indebted to Professor Philip Gammage for his encouragement to write the first edition. His guidance when designing the original research was invaluable.

The many children who took part in the experiments must, of course, remain anonymous but my grateful thanks go out to them.

Thanks must go to Marianne Lagrange whose quiet persuasion and foresight was largely responsible for me writing both the second edition and this new edition.

Above all I am grateful to my dear wife, Anne, for her expertise and professional help on making changes to the text, for her technological guidance and for her understanding while I wrote this third edition instead of accompanying her on the tennis court.

Foreword

In the 1970s Denis Lawrence led the inquiry into the importance of self-esteem for UK educationalists – a topic already acknowledged as significant in the United States. Previously research had focused on raising achievement and then examining whether this improvement resulted in enhanced self-esteem. Lawrence took a different look at this, turning around the quest for a causal relationship between the two. He concentrated on raising self-esteem and demonstrated the resulting improvement in achievement. For the first time an emphasis was put on the importance of a sense of well-being, confidence, security and above all the value of a positive relationship between teacher and pupil.

Amongst his special contributions to the field Lawrence offers a clear and useful definition, describing self-esteem as the degree of match between the sense of self, *self-image*, and the aspirational self, *ideal self*. The practical implications are two-fold:

■ the teacher can concentrate on improving the self image of the student

■ the student and teacher can work together towards achievable aspirations.

Lawrence goes on to offer an extensive menu of activities and strategies to support this approach.

In this edition the very important subject of teacher self-esteem and stress is thoroughly addressed. Teachers face increased challenge to motivate young people who are stimulated by a highly technological and consumer orientated world. They and their families are used to reading or hearing criticism of the teaching profession and publication of comparative data about school performance can undermine the confidence of both teachers and parents.

This edition is published into a new era where self-esteem meets the flourishing popularity of emotional literacy as a significant determining influence on achievement. Those of us who have worked with challenging and underachieving young people are fully aware that poor self-image cannot be 'cured' by lots of praise and high self-esteem alone does not ensure pro-social behaviours, empathy or altruism. Lawrence challenges the recent research by Emler suggesting that high self-esteem is a bad thing, demonstrates that the author does not fully understand the concepts and adequately answers the criticism of self-esteem programmes.

> *It is the development of positive, internalised personal qualities within the child that are the goals of self-esteem enhancement. Self-esteem refers to healthy behaviour, and just as one cannot have too much health, one cannot have too much self-esteem.*

In new sections on the development of integrity, personal responsibility, respect for individual differences, cooperative behaviour, Lawrence sets his work congruently into the context of emotional literacy.

Teachers are significant others – we remember our teachers. We remember whether they diminished us or enabled us. As Lawrence writes,

> *There is no substitute for the enthusiasm, warmth and spontaneity of the personal encounter.*

At the heart of his work is the encouragement to teachers to value the quality of the relationships they have with their students.

It is a confirmation and celebration of the importance and originality of Lawrence's work that this edition is published three decades after his original text and we amongst many others are grateful to him for his important contribution to the British classroom.

Barbara Maines and George Robinson

Introduction

One of the most exciting discoveries in educational psychology in recent times has been the finding that children's levels of achievement and behaviour are influenced by how they feel about themselves. A vast body of research evidence has accumulated showing a positive correlation between these factors.

Perhaps even more exciting has been the practical implications of this research for the classroom teacher. It is clear from the research that teachers are in a powerful position to be able to influence children's self-esteem not only through the use of systematic activities but also through the establishment of particular caring relationships with children. The work of the humanist school of psychology has focused on certain ingredients of personality that are instrumental in this. There is clear evidence that relationships between teachers and children can be either conducive to the enhancement of self-esteem or conducive towards reducing self-esteem.

Whenever the teacher enters into a relationship with a child a process is set in motion which results either in the enhancement of self-esteem or in the reduction of self-esteem. Moreover, this process occurs whether the teacher is aware of it or not. Whilst some teachers may intuitively enhance the self-esteem of children, the evidence is that all teachers might well benefit from an awareness of the principles involved in self-esteem enhancement.

Teaching is more effective when the teacher is able to combine an approach which focuses not only on the development of skills but also on the child's affective state, and on self-esteem in particular. The evidence points to the view that teachers do not have to make a decision whether to teach for skills or self-esteem enhancement – they can do both simultaneously. Indeed, the successful teacher has always combined the behavioural with the affective approach. After all, teaching has traditionally been mainly a process of human interaction.

> BEHAVIOURISM/BEHAVIOURAL. A term originally used by J.B. Watson to denote theories that are concerned with observable behaviour. These theories are in contrast to theories that are concerned primarily with emotions and feelings.

> AFFECTIVE. A term used to describe factors such as emotions and motivation, in contrast to *cognitive* factors such as intelligence and thinking.

Recent developments, however, have tended to focus on the 'non-human' aspects of the teaching process. Developments in high technology and the introduction to schools of the computer have without doubt greatly extended the repertoire of the teacher to the benefit of many children. It is timely to remember that these technological advances were never meant to be substitutes for the teacher. Although technology has an important part to play, the personal interaction between teacher and child should not be minimized. It is through this interaction that children learn to develop interpersonal skills and are helped to develop their self-esteem. There is no substitute for the enthusiasm, warmth and spontaneity of the personal encounter.

Gammage (1986) focuses on this issue when criticizing a then Department of Education and Science circular in Britain on teacher training. There seems to be an official view that teachers should concentrate more on the acquisition of knowledge, reminiscent of 'back to basics' philosophy often expressed in the 1960s, and less on the process of teaching. In the words of Gammage, '*how* teachers teach is as important an issue as *what* they teach'. It is all too easy to be caught up with the traditional behaviourist philosophy with its concentration on the observable behaviour to the exclusion of affective factors.

If the message is so clear, why are so many teachers apparently unaware of the importance of teaching for self-esteem enhancement? One reason could be that the researchers have not easily communicated their findings, and have tended to confuse issues with a lack of consensus on substantive definitions. For instance, English and English (1958) identified over a thousand different combinations and uses of the terms in the self-concept area with the same terms often used to mean different things, and different terms such as *self-esteem, self-concept* and *self-image* often used to mean the same thing. It is not surprising, then, if some teachers have been confused when the researchers themselves have appeared to be unable to define their terms properly. Fortunately this has all begun to come together to the satisfaction of most workers in the self-concept area and the definitions presented in this book are now generally accepted.

> SUBSTANTIVE. An adjective attached to a word, such as self-esteem, to imply that there is recognized evidence for its existence.

> SELF-CONCEPT. This is an umbrella term comprising a person's self-image, ideal self and self-esteem.

> SELF-IMAGE. This is a person's awareness of their mental and physical characteristics.

A second possible reason why teachers have given little prominence to self-esteem enhancement could be the relative absence of guidelines on how to set about the task. Admittedly most teachers are aware of the need to provide positive reinforcements and may be familiar with self-esteem enhancement activities. Those recommended in this book and those suggested by Robinson and Maines (1997), have become popular in many schools. However, teachers have often felt that they have been left with something missing. It is suggested that this missing link is their own part in the process, that is, the qualities of personality of the teacher and their communication skills.

> POSITIVE REINFORCEMENT. This is said to occur when a person's behaviour is rewarded. Positive reinforcement ensures that the behaviour is likely to recur in the future.

Burns (1979b), for instance, drew attention to the way in which the teacher's self-esteem influences the child's self-esteem. Much earlier than this, Rogers (1951) identified the skills of communication which can be learned, and which teachers need to learn to become more effective. Interestingly, the same skills recommended by Rogers are those which are related to the development of the self-concept and associated with successful counselling. These are the skills outlined in this book. The topic will be pursued further not only in connection with the teacher's personality, but also in connection with the communication skills of the teacher outlined in Chapter 6.

The main purpose of this book, therefore, is to help teachers appreciate how they can influence the self-esteem of children in the classroom not only by the quality of their relationships with children, but also through practical activities.

Although the ideas in this book focus mainly on self-esteem and its relationship to achievement and behaviour, the clear corollary is that self-esteem enhancement is a worthwhile teaching aim in its own right. After all, education means more than the learning of academic skills. If we can help children to understand themselves better and to feel more confident about themselves, then they are going to be in a stronger position to be able to cope with the inevitable stresses of life and ultimately to be better citizens. Teachers are in an ideal role to be able to influence this development. Self-esteem enhancement contributes positively towards academic achievement and towards personal and social development.

In our western society, which is so highly competitive, teachers and parents easily become anxious over children's attainments. They are concerned in case the children in their care should fall behind the others. The fact that children learn best when having fun is lost amongst this kind of anxiety. We need to recognize that normal development is a process of coping with the experience of failure and, as teachers, we need to be able to relax and enjoy the child. It is not failure that should be avoided.

Failure is an inevitable part of growing up and the first part of the process of becoming competent. It is only through trial and error that much child learning takes place. The fundamental point here is that whilst failure is an inevitable process, negative criticism need not be. It is not failure which gives concern but the way in which we adults react to failure. The ideal way to react would be to ensure that the child was not being subjected to a situation which was totally beyond his/her level of develop-ment. It would be quite useless, for instance, to expect the normal 3-year-old to be able to cope with a game of chess. Once it has been established that learning a particular task is probably within the child's level of com-petence, then positive steps can be taken.

> LEVEL OF COMPETENCE. This phrase refers to a measured point along a continuum of behaviour. An example of a high level of competence would be a 6-year-old child with a measured reading age of 10 years.

Take, for instance, the child's need to use a knife and fork properly. A first attempt is always a failure – usually with food flying in all directions. At such a time, parents are likely to become irritable, to say the least. Instead of reacting in this way, an effort should be made to come to terms with the behaviour. For example, the utensils could be rearranged so that they are within easier reach, and certainly ensuring that the child practises more and receives plenty of praise at the slightest sign of progress.

These principles apply also in the classroom. If consistently applied, the child will develop confidence to tackle new tasks without associating them with unpleasantness, and he/she is more likely to be eager to learn. This assumes, of course, that the child has received total love and accept-ance from his/her parents – a topic which lies outside this book but which has an equally important part to play in the development of self-esteem.

This book is aimed at both primary and secondary teachers, as the prin-ciples and practices apply from the primary stage to the secondary stage.

Chapter 1 defines the terms self-concept, self-image and ideal self and outlines the development of self-esteem. It also discusses the research evi-dence of a correlation between self-esteem and achievement, indicating the value of organizing self-esteem enhancement programmes in schools.

Chapter 2 examines the role of the total self-concept in self-esteem enhancement programmes. It criticizes some research that casts doubt on the value of self-esteem enhancement programmes and shows how this conclusion is based on a misleading definition of self-esteem. Examples are given of children who may have a faulty self-image and/or a weak ideal self. The question of whether children can have too much self-esteem is raised, showing how this is not possible as self-esteem is defined in this book. The child with the narcissistic personality is contrasted with the child with high self-esteem.

> FAULTY SELF-IMAGE. This term refers to a child's perception of their mental and physical characteristics that is unrealistic and inaccurate.

> NARCISSISTIC PERSONALITY. This term refers to a person with a pathological, unrealistic self-image that gives them an exaggerated sense of their own importance.

> HIGH SELF-ESTEEM. This term refers to a person who is confident and has a realistically positive view of themselves and of their abilities.

Chapter 3 focuses on individual differences in children and the affect of these differences on self-esteem development. Amongst the possible differences discussed are those of physique, ability, gender differences, ethnic differences and problems associated with children who may have special needs.

Chapter 4 examines the significant influences in a child's life, outside the classroom, that affect their self-concept development. The influences examined are family, peers, siblings, sexual identity, race, culture, adolescence and the determining role of the media. The effects of failure experiences outside the school upon self-esteem are examined, emphasizing that it is the attitude towards failure that is the key to self-esteem and not the failure itself.

Chapter 5 looks at the question of assessing self-esteem. It discusses different approaches to measuring self-esteem and reviews some popular methods of assessment of self-esteem. The *Lawseq*, a questionnaire devised by the author and used in the National Child Development Study and standardized on 150,000 children, is recommended for use by teachers. The chapter also discusses the conceptual difficulties involved in measuring self-esteem.

Chapter 6 considers the principles of self-esteem enhancement as an underlying framework to all teaching. This is explained in terms of the need to focus on the quality of the child and teacher relationship. The qualities of acceptance, genuineness and empathy, as identified by Rogers (1975), are discussed as desirable qualities in the teacher.

Chapter 7 outlines a programme of small group activities for children in the classroom. It provides exercises that have been used successfully to enhance self-esteem amongst children with low self-esteem. The aims and rationale of the programme are presented, with suggestions on the selection of children suitable for inclusion in small groups.

ACCEPTANCE. This is a term that describes the quality in a person of being able to respect another person, if not their behaviour. It implies an ability to be non-judgemental of the other person.

EMPATHY. This a personal quality used to describe the ability to experience, reflect and appreciate another person's feelings.

Chapter 8 outlines a programme of whole-class and whole-school activities for the further development of self-esteem. Suggestions are made for their regular inclusion in a school's curriculum.

Chapter 9 outlines individual programmes for self-esteem enhancement. The chapter begins with suggestions for using suitably briefed teaching assistants or non-professional personnel working under the supervision of the teacher. The principles of this approach for working one to one with a child are outlined.

Chapter 10 considers the role of self-esteem in the management of behavioural difficulties in the classroom. Suggestions are made for the management of challenging behaviour that avoid lowering self-esteem.

Chapter 11 introduces self-esteem enhancement as part of a programme to help improve reading attainment in failing readers. The research indicating a positive correlation between self-esteem and reading, conducted by the author, is outlined as evidence for this particular approach. A suggested staged programme for helping children who have reading difficulties is also presented.

Chapter 12 discusses the importance of the teacher's own self-esteem and suggests ways of maintaining high self-esteem in the teacher. It also addresses the problem of stress in teaching and shows how teachers may cope with stress through a structured management programme.

Finally, the Appendix outlines and discusses the author's research findings on which the self-esteem enhancement programmes in this book are based.

What is self-esteem?

▪ CLARIFYING THE TERMINOLOGY ▪

The development of the positive qualities of personal integrity, self-acceptance, respect for the needs of others, and the ability to empathize would comprise the ideal self in a civilized society. It is the development of these ideals that are the goals of a self-esteem enhancement programme as defined in this book. In order to achieve these goals it is important first to clarify the terms used in self-esteem enhancement. We all have our own idea of what we mean by self-esteem, but in any discussion of self-esteem amongst a group of teachers there are likely to be several different definitions. The chances are that amongst these definitions the words *self-concept*, *ideal self* and *self-image* will appear.

The fact is that the literature until fairly recently has tended to use many terms like these to mean the same thing. It is no wonder teachers therefore have been confused and as a result have tended to dismiss the concept as yet another of those ambiguous terms so often found in discussions of education. Fortunately, the concept has gradually been more clearly defined thanks to the work of people like Argyle in Britain and Rogers in the USA.

SELF-CONCEPT

The term *self-concept* is best defined as the sum total of an individual's mental and physical characteristics and his/her evaluation of them. As such it has three aspects: the cognitive (thinking); the affective (feeling); and the behavioural (action). In practice, and from the teacher's point of view, it is useful to consider this self-concept as developing in three areas – self-image, ideal self and self-esteem. Self-esteem, of course, is the focus of this book. To understand the concept of self-esteem, however, it is necessary to define self-image and ideal self.

Self-concept is the umbrella term under which the other three develop. The self-concept is the individual's awareness of his/her own self. It is an awareness of one's own identity. The complexity of the nature of the 'self' has occupied the thinking of philosophers for centuries and was not considered to be a proper topic for psychology until James (1890) resurrected the concept from the realms of philosophy. As with the philosophers of his day, James wrestled with the objective and subjective nature of the 'self – and 'me' and the 'I' – and eventually concluded that it was perfectly reasonable for the psychologist to study the 'self' as an objective phenomenon. He envisaged the infant developing from 'one big blooming buzzing confusion' to the eventual adult state of self-consciousness. The process of development throughout life can be considered, therefore, as a process of becoming more and more aware of one's own characteristics and consequent feelings about them. We see the *self-concept* as an umbrella term (see Figure 1.1) because subsumed beneath the 'self' there are three aspects: self-image (what the person is); ideal self (what the person would like to be); and self-esteem (what the person feels about the discrepancy between what he/she is and what he/she would like to be).

To understand the umbrella nature of the term readers might like to ask themselves the question, 'Who am I?', several times. When first asked, the answer is likely to be name and perhaps sex. When asked a second time the person's job or occupation may be given. The self-image is being revealed so far. Further questioning will lead to the need to reveal more of the person and, in so doing, the ideal self and the self-esteem. For example, 'I am a confident person' (self-esteem); 'I would like to be able to play cricket' (ideal self).

Each of the three aspects of self-concept will be considered in turn. Underpinning this theoretical account of the development of self-concept will be the notion that it is the child's *interpretation* of the life experience which determines self-esteem levels. This is known as the phenomenological approach and owes its origin mainly to the work of Rogers (1951). It attempts to understand a person through empathy with that person and is based on the premise that it is not the events which determine emotions but rather the person's interpretation of the events. To be able to understand the other person requires, therefore, an ability to empathize.

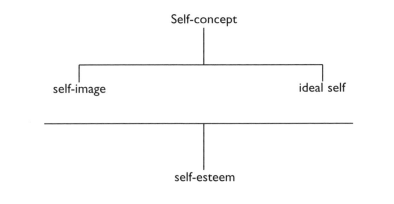

Figure 1.1 *Self-concept as an umbrella term*

SELF-IMAGE

Self-image is the individual's awareness of his/her mental and physical characteristics. It begins in the family with parents giving the child an image of him/herself of being loved or not loved, of being clever or stupid, and so forth, by their non-verbal as well as verbal communication. This process becomes less passive as the child him/herself begins to initiate further personal characteristics. The advent of school brings other experiences for the first time and soon the child is learning that he/she is popular or not popular with other children. He/she learns that school work is easily accomplished or otherwise. A host of mental and physical characteristics are learned according to how rich and varied school life becomes. In fact one could say that the more experiences one has, the richer is the self-image.

The earliest impressions of self-image are mainly concepts of *body-image*. The child soon learns that he/she is separate from the surrounding environment. This is sometimes seen amusingly in the young baby who bites its foot only to discover through pain that the foot belongs to itself. Development throughout infancy is largely a process of this further awareness of body as the senses develop. The image becomes more precise and accurate with increasing maturity so that by adolescence the individual is normally fully aware not only of body shape and size, but also of his/her attractiveness in relation to peers.

Sex-role identity also begins at an early age, probably at birth, as parents and others begin their stereotyping and classifying of the child into one sex or the other. With cognitive development more refined physical and mental skills become possible, including reading and sporting pursuits. These are usually predominant in most schools so that the child soon forms an awareness of his/her capabilities in these areas.

This process of development of the self-image has been referred to as the 'looking-glass theory of self' (Cooley, 1902) as most certainly the individual is forming his/her self-image as he/she receives feedback from others. However, the process is not wholly a matter of 'bouncing *off* the environment' but also one of 'reflecting *on* the environment' as cognitive abilities make it possible for individuals to reflect on their experiences and interpret them.

Self-image is our starting point for an understanding of self-esteem.

IDEAL SELF

Side by side with the development of self-image the child is learning that there are ideal characteristics he/she should possess – that there are ideal standards of behaviour and particular skills which are valued. For example, adults place value on being clean and tidy, and 'being clever' is important. As with self-image, the process begins in the family and continues on entry to school. Once they attend school they would normally learn that teachers also value the kind of behaviour valued by their parents. Not only are they praised for behaving appropriately, but they also receive rewards and positive feedback from their teachers when they learn to read and to write. In this way, praise becomes a goal and provides them with motivation for further appropriate behaviour and achievements.

Further development of the ideal self occurs as children come into contact with the standards and values of people outside the family and the school. The child is becoming aware of the mores of the society. Body-image, again, is one of the earliest impressions of the ideal self as parents comment on the shape and size of their child. Soon the child is comparing him/herself with others and eventually with peers. Peer comparisons are particularly powerful at adolescence. The influence of the media also becomes a significant factor at this time with various advertising and show-business personalities providing models of aspiration. Role models in the media often have a powerful influence although it is usually the people closest to them that continue to have the strongest influence. However, it is the positive qualities of empathy and respect for others, and a sense of personal responsibility that ought to be the ideal goals of people in a civilized society. So the ideal self does not merely comprise the values and standards of the person's immediate social group but, rather, the ideals and standards of a larger civilized society.

With maturity a person's total experiences are able to be evaluated more realistically, although it is doubtful whether a person ever becomes sufficiently mature to be completely uninfluenced. Our early experiences may continue to influence our present behaviour to some extent although we all have the potential for becoming self-determinate. The schoolchild is most likely to be at the stages of accepting these ideal images from the significant people around him/her and of striving to a greater or lesser degree to attain them.

SELF-ESTEEM

Self-esteem is the individual's *evaluation* of the discrepancy between self-image and ideal self. From the discussion on the development of self-image and ideal self it can be appreciated that the discrepancy between the two is inevitable and so can be regarded as a normal phenomenon.

Self-esteem can be either global or specific and there is a relationship between these two facets of self-esteem. Global self-esteem refers to an all-round feeling of self-worth and confidence. Specific self-esteem refers to a feeling of self-worth and confidence with regard to a specific activity or behaviour.

If a particular activity or behaviour is valued, the chances are that eventually it will affect a person's global self-esteem. For instance, a child may have an overall feeling of positive self-worth, that is, high global self-esteem, but feel inadequate when having to play sport. If sport is highly valued in this school, their global self-esteem will be threatened. However, if sport is not valued in their school, their global self-esteem may remain unaffected. Even if a regular activity such as sport is valued and the child fails at this, it should still be possible to maintain high self-esteem by avoiding sport. This strategy of avoiding specific activities is more easily accomplished in adult life than in the school situation. It is difficult to avoid school activities, especially when they are so often compulsory. An example of such an activity would be learning to read.

In the process of normal development there is always a discrepancy between self-image and ideal self. It is this discrepancy that motivates people to change or to develop social, physical and academic skills. However, in some cases, adults might be anxious about their child's slow progress. They may communicate their disapproval of the fact that the child has not yet reached their ideal. Sadly, the child usually interprets this criticism as not just disapproval over their failure in the activity concerned but disapproval of them as a person. Consequently, these children also become extremely anxious about their failure to meet the adult's standards and, so, their global self-esteem drops.

Indeed, there is evidence from clinical work that without this discrepancy – without levels of aspiration – individuals can become apathetic and poorly adjusted. Just as in physiology the nerve impulse is always active so, it seems, the psyche also needs to be active. It is a mistake to think that the ideal state is one of total relaxation. Whilst this may be desirable for a short while, in the long run it can produce neurotic behaviour. For the person to be striving is therefore a normal state.

What is not normal is that the individual should worry and become distressed over the discrepancy. Clearly, this is going to depend in early child-hood on how the significant people in the child's life react to him/her. For instance, if the parent is overanxious about the child's development this will soon be communicated and the child, too, will also become overanxious about it. He/she begins first by trying to fulfil the parental expectations, but if he/she is not able to meet them begins to feel guilty.

It is interesting that the young child is so trusting in the adults that he/she does not consider that they could be wrong or misguided. When a child fails to live up to parental expectations he/she blames him/herself at first, feeling unworthy of their love. Moreover, this failure in a particular area generalizes so that he/she would not just feel a failure, say, in reading attainment, but will feel a failure as a person generally. The child is not able to compartmentalize his/her life as can the adult. If we adults cannot play chess, for instance, we avoid the chess club. If the child fails in, say, reading, he/she cannot avoid the situation.

Indeed, the subject of reading is probably the most important skill he/she will learn in the primary school and normally will come into con-tact with reading every day of school life. It is not surprising therefore that the child who fails in reading over a lengthy period should be seen to have developed low self-esteem, the end product of feeling guilt about his/her failure. The child then lacks confidence in him/herself.

It can be appreciated from the foregoing description of the develop-ment of self-concept that teachers are in a very strong position to be able to influence self-esteem. It should be pointed out perhaps at this juncture that not all children who fail in school work will have low self-esteem. Those parents, and sometimes those teachers, who put no pressure at all on the child to achieve will not, of course, be worrying the child over his/her failure. But at the same time, without some demands being made on the child, he/she will not likely be achieving.

The rule is: unrealistic demands may result in low self-esteem, but no demands at all may result in no achievement. Clearly, there must be an optimum amount of pressure – just enough to cause the child to care but not too much so that he/she becomes distressed. The secret is to be aware of the child's present level of functioning so that our demands to extend this level will be realistic. In the area of language development, for instance, we should not normally expect our child to be able to use a long, complex sentence structure until his/her span of attention and memory-span have developed sufficiently to be able to retain it. It can be appreciated at once that the child's present level of functioning in any area is likely to depend on a complex interrelatedness of many factors. Only an intimate knowledge of the child will give us this information.

It is not the failure to achieve that produces low self-esteem; it is the way the significant people in the child's life react to the failure. Indeed, it could be argued that failure is an inevitable part of life and, indeed, trial-and-error learning can be an effective method of learning in certain circumstances. Failure need not be feared. After all, there is always someone cleverer or more skilled than ourselves. This must be accepted if we are to help children develop happily without straining always to be on top. Eventually, of course, children become aware of their own level of achievement and realize that they are not performing as well as others around them. Then they can develop low self-esteem irrespective of the opinions of others; they have set their own standards. It is probably true to say, however, that the primary school child is still likely to be 'internalizing' his/her ideal self from the significant people around him/her. These people, of course, can include peers as well as teachers and family.

Children who have received a realistic self-image and an ideal self that are consistent with the mores of their particular society should arrive at school with high self-esteem. They will have confidence in themselves, be emotionally and socially well adjusted and eager for new experiences.

■ HOW SELF-ESTEEM OPERATES ■

The child with high self-esteem is likely to be confident in social situations and in tackling school work. He/she will have retained a natural curiosity for learning and will be eager and enthusiastic when presented with a new challenge.

The child with low self-esteem, in contrast, will lack confidence in his/her ability to succeed. Consequently, he/she may try to avoid situations which he/she sees as potentially personally humiliating. In the words of the famous philosopher and psychologist, William James (1890), 'With no attempt there can be no failure; with no failure no humiliation'. This explains why some students prefer to do nothing even though knowing they are likely to incur the teacher's displeasure. To be punished and perhaps be seen as something of a hero by their peers is better than to be seen to be foolish.

AVOIDANCE AND COMPENSATION

Depending on whether the child is by temperament inclined to extroversion or introversion, he/she will meet the situation with avoidance or an attempt to compensate. If inclined to extroversion he/she is more likely to compensate and fight back at the source of the frustration. So we can have the child who is arrogant and boastful on the surface, and so giving an impression of anything but low self-esteem. At its extreme this would be the classical 'inferiority complex', a phrase first used by Jung (1923). On the other hand, if introverted by temperament, the child is more likely to withdraw and demonstrate the shy, timid behaviour which common sense immediately tells us is an indication of low self-esteem.

In both cases the child is avoiding the feeling of failure. Clearly, if he/she avoids work the teacher is going to be alerted, but more often than not, this then takes the form of exhorting the child to 'get down and do some work' or even a mental note that 'this child is lazy'. It can be appreciated, however, that the child is merely communicating that he/she would rather risk the wrath of the teacher than suffer the feeling of humiliation which he/she sees as the inevitable consequence of tackling new work.

The question is: why is humiliation so terrible and to be avoided at all costs? To answer this question we turn to the humanistic psychologists, of whom the best known, perhaps, is Carl Rogers (1961). Carl Rogers has drawn our attention to the prime need in our culture for self-regard. In a society where generally people no longer starve, and where primitive drives are easily expressed, it seems that our most important need is to preserve self-esteem. Whether this is innate or learned does not matter. We all need to be liked and to be valued. When we cannot fulfil this need easily we tend to identify this with material things which we know will be admired and so set out to possess as large a car or as large a house as we can. Or, we may divert this need into our children, not just by basking in their achievement, but sometimes misguidedly living out our own lives through them.

MOTIVATION

A second phenomenon of the self-concept is that it is a motivator. We all tend to behave in ways which fit in with our perception of ourselves. Indeed, we can feel decidedly insecure when we are expected to behave in a manner which we might regard as 'not me'. One example of this would be the shy, low self-esteem child who is suddenly called upon to read the address at the school assembly in front of perhaps 400 others. Consider also the student teacher facing a class for the first time. Both are going to feel very anxious indeed.

> MOTIVATOR. This term, in reference to the self-concept, implies that the self-concept determines the direction of a person's behaviour. For instance, a child whose self-concept tells them that they are good readers will be attracted to a library. The child whose self-concept tells them that they are poor readers will tend to avoid a library.

At a less dramatic level, but none the less important, is the retarded reader who daydreams during the school library sessions. He/she does not see reading as relevant to his/her self-concept. Reading is for the 'clever ones'. Even though the child may comply with the teacher's demand to read he/she would just 'go through the motions' of reading without really being highly motivated. This would mean, of course, that any learning which did take place would not be retained in the long term. This child can baffle the teacher as he/she seems to learn in the short term. In addition he/she seems to possess all the skills necessary to make progress. Often, these children score well in intelligence tests and show no perceptual difficulties, neither do they show overt signs of emotional disturbance. However, without attention to their low self-esteem they are not likely to make long-term progress.

RESISTANCE

A third important feature of self-concept is that it tends to be resistant to change. This means that we cannot reasonably expect our failing reader suddenly to see him/herself as a potentially good reader, even with therapeutic intervention. It can be quite threatening for a child with learning difficulties to be informed that he/she will soon be 'clever' and be able to read. It needs to be a gradual process.

It seems that it is just 'human nature' to want to maintain self-consistency. It is quite startling to meet people with the most severe of handicaps desperately clinging to their handicaps in the face of a possible change. We need to know who we are, and the familiar is safer than the unfamiliar even if known to be inadequate. The hearing-impaired person may resist at first any surgery which can restore the hearing merely because of the risk to self-concept. This is not meant to suggest he/she would not eventually go through with an operation but it is not an easy decision to make when it also means changing the self-concept.

The low self-esteem person is even more resistant to change as it means taking risks which he/she cannot easily do in the sense of either learning new skills or being a different person. Any remedial approach to the child with a learning difficulty should therefore take this factor into account.

■ THE SELF-ESTEEM HIERARCHY ■

The question often posed is 'Can we have low self-esteem in one situation and high self-esteem in another?' It is only asked by those who have not understood the hierarchical nature of self-esteem (Shavelson *et al.*, 1976).

Self-esteem as defined so far refers to a 'global self-esteem' – an individual's overall feeling of self-worth. This is relatively stable and consistent over time. In addition to this overall, or global, self-esteem we can have feelings of worth or unworthiness in specific situations. Accordingly, we may feel inadequate (low self-esteem) with regard to mathematics or tennis playing. However, they do not affect our overall feeling of self-worth as we can escape their influences by avoiding those situations. If, of course, we cannot avoid them and regularly participate in these activities which make us feel inadequate, they may eventually affect our overall self-esteem. Also, if we continue to fail in areas which are valued by the significant people in our lives then our overall self-esteem is affected. It is worth reflecting on how children cannot escape school subjects which is why failure in school so easily generalizes to the global self-esteem.

> GLOBAL SELF-ESTEEM. This term refers to a person's overall feeling of self-worth as opposed to *specific* self-esteem that refers to a person's feeling of self-worth in regard to a specific activity or skill.

It is important to appreciate this hierarchy of self-esteem as confusion often arises when people make statements such as 'Girls have lower self-esteem than boys'. This is not borne out by the research if we are referring to global self-esteem (Marsh *et al.*, 1984), but it is true when referring to mathematics and science. Even here we must be careful to distinguish between statistical significance and practical significance. The research mentioned refers to statistical significance but the differences *within* the sexes are greater so that, practically, we can say there are no real differences between the sexes. Figure 1.2 illustrates the self-esteem hierarchy (Shavelson and Bolus, 1982)

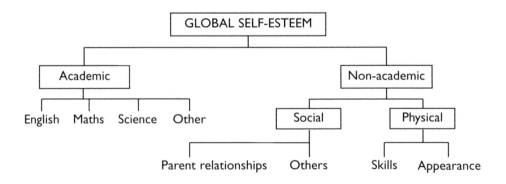

Figure 1.2 *The self-esteem hierarchy*

Summarizing the development of self-esteem, the process begins with interpersonal relationships within the family which gradually give precedence to school influences and to the influences of the larger society in which the individual chooses to live and work. These extraneous influences lose their potency to the extent to which the individual becomes self-determinate. For the child of school age, however, self-esteem continues to be affected mainly by the significant people in the life of the child, usually parents, teachers and peers.

INTERPERSONAL RELATIONSHIPS. This term refers to the face-to-face social interactions that exist between people in a group situation.

SELF-DETERMINATE. A person who is self-determinate is able to choose to behave in a particular way because they have made an independent decision to do so. This is contrasted with the person who is not self-determinate and whose behaviour is determined for them by other people.

■ THE EVIDENCE FOR SELF-ESTEEM ENHANCEMENT ■

The need to maintain children's self-esteem is self-evident and most teachers are well aware of the importance of the value attached to helping children feel good about themselves. On common-sense grounds one would expect children with high self-esteem to do better in class than children with low self-esteem. And this is supported by the research which consistently shows a positive correlation between children's self-esteem and their levels of attainment. The correlational studies usually reveal a figure around 0.6, which indicates that other factors are also relevant in whether children achieve or not. Obviously, ability is an essential factor in the achievement equation. However, it is clear from the research that children will not use their full ability if their self-esteem is low. This is well documented in research carried out by the author and also in other more recently published research (Rosenburg *et al.*, 1995; Mrak, 1999, Crocker and Wolfe, 2001; Galbraith and Alexander, 2005). Davies and Brember (1999), reporting the results of an eight-year cross-sectional study measuring self-esteem, showed significant correlations between self-esteem and all their attainment scores.

It is over 25 years since the first of a long series of experiments was begun by the author in Somerset, England, into the enhancement of children's self-esteem. The original experiments concluded that teachers were able to enhance children's self-esteem over a six-month period through a systematic programme of individual self-esteem enhancement. This research is discussed in more detail in Appendix 1.

Following these experiments it was hypothesized that the results were a function of the quality of the relationships established and not necessarily dependent on either the academic or professional qualifications of the author. If this were the case it should be possible for non-professionals to obtain the same results. A further series of experiments were then conducted using non-professionals. They were briefed on self-concept theory as outlined above and shown how to organize the sessions.

They were seen to obtain the same results as a professional psychologist. It was becoming clear that the essential ingredient in the process was the communication skills of the people conducting the programme, as discussed in Chapter 9. The conclusion from these experiments was not that teachers or psychologists were unsuited to this task. Indeed, on common-sense grounds, with their training and knowledge of children, they should be even more skilled than non-professionals. The significant conclusion was that no matter what the professional qualifications of the people conducting the programme, they would not be effective unless they also possessed the qualities of personality which the research shows to be essential. Brief details of these experiments are given in Appendix 1.

The results of the above experiments were later translated into workshops for teachers. The author was invited by the Western Australian Government Ministry of Education to conduct self-esteem workshops throughout that state and over 200 schools were eventually served. Following the publication of the results of this research many schools in the United Kingdom began to appreciate the significance of a self-esteem programme.

The research evidence does not point only to the positive correlation between self-esteem and academic achievement. There is also evidence of a positive correlation between self-esteem and children's behaviour. It seems that children with high self-esteem are more likely to get on better with others and so have fewer behaviour problems. In the experiments reported, teachers regularly mentioned a reduction in behavioural difficulties amongst those who had been on the self-esteem programme, although this was not the main object of the programme. The self-esteem enhancement programme was more modest in its aims, merely trying to help children change their attitudes towards themselves. Not all children who have low self-esteem have behavioural difficulties. The fact that the self-esteem experiments did not specifically aim to reduce behavioural difficulties is important in highlighting the similarities and differences between a self-esteem programme and one aimed to help children who do show behavioural difficulties. The latter are discussed in more detail in Chapter 10. However, it should be mentioned that research concludes that when a teacher is faced with children showing behavioural difficulties, no matter what sanctions or disciplinary measures the teacher may decide to use, the manner in which they are used is crucial with regard to the child's self-esteem. Also, research concludes that self-esteem enhancement need not by any means be inconsistent with good discipline in the classroom. Children in any context who know where the boundaries to their behaviour lie, and how far they can go, generally feel more secure and are usually of higher self-esteem. The famous research of Stanley Coopersmith (1967) into behaviour and attitudes, although conducted over 25 years ago, is just as valid today.

Self-esteem enhancement does not mean always that focus has to be on helping children feel good about themselves. Some children are so immature that they are still relatively unconscious of themselves and often the best way to help them is to try to help them become more aware of their behaviour. Ask these children why they behaved in a particular way and they usually answer 'I don't know'. This can infuriate the adult asking the question but it is generally the case that they genuinely do not know. For them any programme of self-esteem enhancement should be postponed until they are aware of a self to be enhanced. Perhaps one of the most startling of research findings is the conclusion that there is a correlation between children's self-esteem and teacher self-esteem. Children of high self-esteem who are in regular contact with teachers of low self-esteem will gradually themselves develop low self-esteem, with associated low attainment levels. On a more positive note, the converse can also occur, with low self-esteem children raising their self-esteem through regular contact with high self-esteem teachers (Burns, 1982).

It is clear from all the research that teachers are in a powerful position to influence children's self-esteem and in turn influence their achievements and behaviour. Perhaps most teachers are already aware of this, and probably already enhance children's self-esteem intuitively. However, a knowledge of the research, together with familiarity with self-concept theory would provide teachers with a proper rationale so that they are in a position to know how to go about enhancing self-esteem systematically.

The research would suggest that teachers can enhance self-esteem in three ways:

1. Through a systematic programme of group activities lasting usually a term. These are described in Chapters 7 and 8.

2. Through an individual self-esteem enhancement programme. This is discussed further in Chapter 9.

3. Through providing a positive ethos in the classroom. This is probably the most usual way in which teachers influence children's self-esteem. This is the method which is more likely to be done on an intuitive basis. The self-esteem and communication skills of the teacher are the significant factors in this process, as discussed in Chapter 6. Teachers can either reduce or enhance children's self-esteem according to how they manage the general ethos of the classroom.

Self-esteem enhancement does not have to take the form of a systematic programme. The opinion has been expressed in some quarters that teachers do not always have time for self-esteem enhancement. This view is based on a false premise of what self-esteem enhancement is about. All teaching should be carried out within a generally self-esteem enhancing framework. This means the teacher establishing positive relationships with the children in their care. Suggestions and guidance for establishing positive relationships in the classroom are discussed in Chapter 6.

■ FURTHER READING ■

Crocker, J. and Wolfe, C.T. (2001) Contingencies of self-worth, *Psychological Review*, Vol. 108, pp. 593–623.

Davies, J. and Brember, I. (1999) Reading and mathematics attainments and self-esteem in Years 2 and 6 – an eight year cross-sectional study, *Educational Studies*, Vol. 25, pp. 145–57.

Dewhurst, D. (1991) Should teachers enhance their pupils' self-esteem?, *Journal of Moral Education*, Vol. 20, no. 1, pp. 3–11.

Galbraith, A. and Alexander, J. (2005) Literacy self-esteem and locus of control, *Support for Learning*, Vol. 20, no. 1, pp. 28–34.

Greenhalgh, P. (1994) *Emotional Growth and Learning*, London, Routledge.

Marston, A.R. (1986) Dealing with low self-confidence, *Educational Research*, Vol. 10, pp. 134–8.

Mrak, C.J. (1999) *Self-Esteem, Research, Theory and Practice (1999)*, 2nd edn, New York, Springer, pp. 141–56.

Rosenburg, M. (1995) Global self-esteem and specific self-esteem: different concepts, different outcomes, *American Sociological Review*, Feb, Vol. 60, pp. 141–56.

Stevens, R. (ed.) (1995) *Understanding the Self*, London, Sage.

The role of the self-concept in self-esteem enhancement

Throughout this book a self-concept theory approach to teaching has been advocated. The principles underpinning this approach were outlined and discussed in the previous chapter. Self-concept theory views the individual's personality as comprising the three components of self-image, ideal self and self-esteem. The various techniques and strategies for enhancing self-esteem in the classroom validated in the author's original research were presented. Other researchers have since corroborated this research so that there is now persuasive evidence for this approach (Davies and Brember, 1999). Davies and Brember, reporting the results of an eight-year cross-sectional study measuring self-esteem, showed significant correlations between self-esteem and all their attainment scores.

However, there are some teachers who have applied the self-esteem enhancement techniques recommended and have questioned this approach. It seems that they may require further convincing of the value of self-esteem enhancement programmes.

There are several possible reasons why a specific self-esteem enhancement programme may appear to some teachers not to work, but the most likely reason may be a misunderstanding over the nature of self-esteem. It is important to recognize that self-esteem is only one component in a child's total self-concept. Although the focus of a self-esteem enhancement programme is naturally on strategies designed to enhance the child's self-esteem, the other two elements of the self-concept, self-image and ideal self, often have important parts to play in this process.

In reported instances of a self-esteem enhancement programme appearing not to work, it is probable that the other elements of the child's total self-concept have not been addressed. An analysis of the development of the child's self-concept would probably reveal that the failure of the self-esteem programme is likely to have been due either to the weak development of the child's ideal self or because the child had a distorted self-image. In some instances, both the child's ideal self and the child's self-image should have received attention before addressing the child's self-esteem. Strategies for developing a realistic self-image and a socially acceptable ideal self are discussed in Chapters 7 and 8.

The ideal development of the self-concept was described in Chapter 1. Unfortunately, some children do not have this ideal development. As a result, any of the three elements of the self-concept, self-image, ideal self or self-esteem, may remain undeveloped in some children. The ways in which this happens and their effects on behaviour are discussed in this chapter but first it is important to repeat the meaning of self-esteem and to correct any misapprehensions over its use.

■MISAPPREHENSION OVER THE NATURE OF SELF-ESTEEM■

Despite the research evidence showing the value of self-esteem enhancement programmes, they have recently been under scrutiny in some schools and the value of the programmes has been debated. The view has been expressed in some schools that children these days often have too much self-esteem. This view appeared to be supported by some research purporting to show that children have too much self-esteem (Bushman and Baumeister, 1998; Elmer, 2001).

Elmer (2001) reviewed research literature on self-esteem and concluded that low self-esteem was not a factor in either academic achievement or delinquency. Furthermore, parents and teachers were criticized in the conclusions from this research for trying to enhance self-esteem by using praise indiscriminately.

These are serious criticisms of the value of self-esteem programmes as well as of parents and teachers who implement such programmes. Such criticism should not remain unchallenged. As Branden (1999) has reported, the use of praise in this way does not reflect an adequate understanding of self-esteem. Even more to the point, Elmer's research appears to be an example of a common misunderstanding over exactly what is meant by self-esteem enhancement. As described in Chapter 1, self-esteem enhancement is not merely about unabated praise to make children feel good about themselves. Randomly praising children is a reliance on an external method of control and signifies a very simplistic notion of what is meant by self-esteem enhancement.

Self-esteem enhancement involves addressing the total self-concept. This often means having to pay attention to the development of the child's self-image and their ideal self. As previously stated, enhancing self-esteem means much more than just routinely praising children and/or their work, whether planning a self-esteem enhancement framework to teaching or devising a specific self-esteem enhancement programme. It is the development of positive, internalized personal qualities within the child that are the goals of self-esteem enhancement. Self-esteem refers to healthy behaviour, and just as one cannot have too much health, one cannot have too much self-esteem.

Whilst there is a place for genuine praise in self-esteem enhancement, this has to be realistic praise, otherwise the child will be in danger of developing a faulty self-image. This is not meant to denigrate the use of praise during teaching. When used judiciously, praise can be a powerful motivator to children. However, children would become habituated to continual praise so that eventually it would lose its effect. External factors such as praise or other types of material reward always lose their effectiveness in the long run.

As defined in Chapter 1, the development of high self-esteem in the child is not dependent, in the long term, on external factors. Sustained high self-esteem is dependent on *internal* factors such as feelings of confidence and personal integrity and not on *external* factors like praise. While praise may initially establish a positive environment for self-esteem enhancement, especially when given appropriately and realistically, ultimately, high self-esteem is dependent on the child forming his/her own values and standards. Thus, high self-esteem is best regarded as a function of *implicit* self-attitudes and not of *explicit* ones.

■ CAN CHILDREN HAVE TOO MUCH SELF-ESTEEM? ■

It can be appreciated why self-esteem may sometimes have been considered in a negative sense. Children who are disruptive in the classroom often appear to be extremely confident and may seem to be little troubled by the effects of their behaviour. These are the children who have sometimes been referred to as having too much self-esteem. A more thorough assessment of their problem behaviour often reveals that they have underlying low self-esteem and are far from being confident. They may have feelings of inadequacy that they try to mask by outwardly confident behaviour. This has often been described as 'pseudo self-esteem'. Pseudo self-esteem has its source in external factors such as praise and admiration. If these external sources disappear their self-esteem drops. Management of this type of behaviour would begin by identifying the sources of the child's inadequate feelings. Once the reasons for their low self-esteem are apparent an appropriate remedial programme could be offered.

A question that is sometimes asked is 'why is it a child can have behavioural problems and may even be failing in school work yet can still have high self-esteem?' Once again, reference to the child's total self-concept provides the answer. The apparent paradox lies in an analysis of the child's self-image, their ideal-self and their self-esteem. A child may be found to have undeveloped or distorted beliefs in any one or more areas of self-concept. This type of child may have not been able to develop a self-concept in the ideal way, as discussed in Chapter 1. For various reasons they may have developed a totally unrealistic ideal self and also an unrealistic self-image. What has become known as the *narcissistic* personality would come under this heading.

A narcissistic person has a grandiose view of themselves as being superior and unique (Lowen, 2004). They have such an inflated sense of self-regard that they become preoccupied with being admired by others. Most psychiatrists would probably regard this as a personality disorder but it could also be regarded as being at the end of a continuum of behaviour. Fortunately, this condition is rare.

The following sections illustrate why it is sometimes necessary also to address the child's ideal self and/or their self-image in a self-esteem enhancement programme.

▣ THE CHILD WITH THE UNDEVELOPED SELF-IMAGE ▣

One of the reasons for challenging behaviour in a child who appears to have high self-esteem might be an undeveloped self-image. It is normal for children to be egocentric during the infant stage but some children remain at this early stage of development. There would be little use embarking on a self-esteem enhancement programme for this type of child. Exercises and strategies would need to be implemented that focus in the first instance on helping the child to develop more of an awareness of themselves.

> EGOCENTRIC. This term refers to behaviour that is concerned wholly with the satisfaction of a person's own needs. The process of social development in children is one of gradually becoming less egocentric.

Newborn babies begin life totally egocentric and unaware of themselves physically or mentally. As they develop they gradually learn that they are separate from their environment and eventually that they have a physical being. Through normal communication with their parents, children gradually become aware of themselves. Once in school this process accelerates and children learn a host of things about themselves. As they communicate with others they become aware of their physical, social and mental abilities.

Unfortunately, some children do not easily learn their real characteristics from their parents. The family environment may be chaotic with little opportunity for one-to-one relationships. For example, there may be some families with a continual high noise level such as loud music playing, television blaring, raised conflictual voices, dogs barking and machinery running. Children in families like this may have a poorly developed self-image. They behave instinctively, without a capacity for reflection, and consequently they remain relatively unaware of themselves. Stott (1966) was the first to identify this kind of personality development when investigating delinquency. He referred to this type of child as being 'inconsequential'. Such children tend to act first and think second.

> INCONSEQUENTIAL. This is a term used to describe behaviour in some children that occurs without reference to its possible consequences. Children who are inconsequential are unable to delay gratification.

Strategies for managing disruptive behaviour in this child with an underdeveloped self-image depend on the age of the child. It would be normal to find children at the infant stage with underdeveloped self-images. Infant teachers are used to having to help children develop their self-images. They usually begin by helping the children develop a sense of their physical image as described in Chapter 3.

The older child who shows an underdeveloped self-image will require a different approach. It would usually be possible to discuss their behaviour with older children and so help them to reflect on their self-image. There would be two aims to this approach. The first would be for the child to take responsibility for his/her behaviour and the second would be to help him/her understand the benefits of behaving properly. This would need to be done within a non-judgemental empathic approach as discussed in Chapter 6. The process is likely to need several sessions, so again it may be advisable to refer the case to the educational psychologist.

Some children who have only a vague awareness of their self-image may have experienced very constricting childhood experiences. This means that they will lack practice in coping with their environment. Where children are sheltered from experiences such as playing with other children, they find it hard when first entering school and having to mix with other children. Once again, depending on the age of the child, the aim should be to help him/her understand the effects of his/her behaviour and to take responsibility for it.

■ THE CHILD WITH THE UNREALISTIC SELF-IMAGE ■

There is evidence for the self-image as a motivator. People generally feel uneasy unless allowed to behave in ways that fit in with their image of themselves. So, for instance, if a person is suddenly expected to take the lead in a meeting when they perceive themselves to be a follower, they begin to feel uneasy. Children with an unrealistic self-image are equally uneasy when expected in school to behave in different ways from their image of themselves.

Most children arrive at school with a realistic idea of the kind of person they are. However, there are other children who come from families where children have developed an image of themselves that is a totally unrealistic one. They feel that they know the kind of people they are and that they are aware of their abilities, but their awareness of themselves is unrealistic. These children are often described as having developed a 'pseudo' or 'faulty' self-image.

A detailed assessment of this child's difficulties usually reveals that they have an exaggerated sense of their own importance. This child can present an even bigger challenge to the teacher than the child with the underlying feelings of inadequacy, especially as the child reaches adolescence. Adolescents are noted for their search for identity and for being self-conscious. If, in addition, they have an exaggerated sense of their own importance, there would be the danger at the adult stage of assuming a narcissistic personality.

There can be several reasons for the development of a faulty self-image but in young children it is sometimes the result of parental overindulgence. For instance, some children may have regularly been told by their parents that they are cleverer than other children, or that that they are unusually gifted. They may have had very few demands made on them at home. Another example would be the child with a particular health problem. With good intentions the parents may have relaxed certain attitudes and expectations for the child, not wishing to exacerbate the child's condition. Children like this inevitably lack the necessary practice of behaving independently and so can be over-demanding of the teacher's time.

Additionally, the child who has been regularly told by their parents that they are unusually gifted would arrive at school expecting more atten-tion than is given to the other children. With this belief about themselves they would find it difficult to make friends with other children. As well as being over-demanding of the teacher's time, they often resent having to share their teacher with the other children in the class, leading to an accompanying risk of developing low self-esteem. The average child who has an unrealistic self-image that conveys that he/she is unusually gifted intellectually will eventually find that there are other children who are often cleverer than them. They are likely to become anxious when they dis-cover their true abilities. This can lead either to a lack of confidence in themselves or they quickly develop low self-esteem.

Children with a faulty self-image are unprepared for the normal hurly-burly of the classroom and the playground. When other people do not respond to them in the same way as their parents have related to them, this can cause them anxiety and other kinds of behavioural problems can occur, such as refusing to attend school. It is not surprising that away from the family these children are at risk of developing behavioural difficulties with the added risk of developing low self-esteem.

In contrast to children who may have been highly praised by their teachers, there are others with a faulty self-image who may have been told regularly by their parents that they are stupid, when in fact testing in school may show that they are above average in ability. These children come to school with little enthusiasm for class work and usually under-perform. Unless this behaviour is investigated by the teacher these children will always underperform in academic work. As with the child who has an inflated image of him/herself, the child with this kind of faulty self-image would usually also show behavioural difficulties.

■ THE CHILD WITH THE WEAK IDEAL SELF ■

For various reasons, some children have not been helped at home to develop an ideal self so they arrive at school with very little idea of how to behave and with very little motivation to achieve. They show behavioural problems simply because they know no better responses to the situation in which they find themselves. It may be that they have different social and cultural values from those of the school in which they have been placed. They may fail in school work simply because they have not yet learned that there are advantages in achieving success in education. Their ideal self does not comprise the values of the school.

Children with these difficulties have a hard time learning acceptable behaviour and learning that there is satisfaction in academic achievement. These children usually present the biggest challenge to the teacher in the classroom. They are often unruly and disruptive in class.

The first challenge for the teacher is how best to begin to help these children develop their ideal self that would be consistent with the values and standards of their school. The development of the long-term goals of self-responsibility, empathy, and the ability to cooperate and have respect for the needs of others may well have to take second place. The development of an ideal self in a child is not an easy task and it can require the cooperation of the parents to help modify their attitudes towards the child. The task is made even more difficult if the standards and values of the parents are different from those of the child's school. However, it is still possible to help the child with unacceptable behaviour in the specific classroom environment, although there can be no guarantee that the improved behaviour will generalize to situations outside the classroom. Successful modification of the child's ideal self will not only depend upon the cooperation of the parents, but also the extent to which the teacher can be empathetic and non-judgemental of the child.

It may be necessary for the teacher to introduce an individual self-esteem programme, as described in Chapter 9, to help a child develop an ideal self. However, when the child is deliberately flouting the school rules and is rude to the teacher an appeal to reason is usually doomed to failure. The only way to deal with this problem in the early stages is through a behavioral conditioning programme in order to establish a pattern of appropriate behavior. It may be unlikely that some children, with a weak ideal self, would respond to a self-esteem enhancement programme without also receiving intensive psychological treatment. The educational psychologist would normally be asked to devise a behaviour modification programme in the more serious cases. This would involve the application of incentives and rewards for appropriate behaviour. Depending on the seriousness of the child's behaviour difficulties, the programme might also require the application of particular constraints.

Once a pattern of appropriate behaviour has been established a self-esteem enhancement approach might be advocated. The ultimate aims would be to help the child develop an ideal self consistent with the values of the school and, eventually, become responsible for their own behaviour. Their chances of success would depend very much on the teacher receiving support and guidance from the psychologist as well as support from the child's parents.

In conclusion, self-esteem enhancement programmes do work. There is ample research evidence for this to recommend that they should be part of every school's curriculum. They have been seen not only to reduce the incidence of behavioural problems in the classroom, but also to increase children's academic attainments. However, it is important to be clear on exactly what is meant by self-esteem before embarking on such a pro-gramme. Sometimes it may be necessary first to have knowledge of the development of the child's total self-concept. The child's self-image and/or ideal self may need to be addressed before beginning a self-esteem enhancement programme. The child with the unrealistic self-image would need help in becoming more aware of him/herself and may also have an undeveloped ideal self that should be developed.

Finally, self-esteem enhancement programmes are not designed merely to help children feel good about themselves. They are designed to help children develop a sense of responsibility for their behaviour, develop the ability to empathize with others and to have respect for the needs of others as well as developing a sense of personal worth.

■ FURTHER READING ■

Barry, C., Frick, P. and Killian, A. (2003) The relation of narcissism and self-esteem conduct problems in children: a preliminary investigation, *Journal of Clinical Child and Adolescent Psychology*, Vol. 32, no. 1, pp. 139–52.

Baumeister, R.F., Smart, L. and Boden, J.M. (1996) Reaction of threatened egotism to violence and aggression: the dark side of high self-esteem, *Psychological Review*, pp. 1035–7.

Covington, M. (1989) *Self-esteem and Failure In School: The Social Importance of Self-esteem*, Berkeley, CA, UCA.

Emler, N. (2001) *Self-esteem: The Costs and Causes of Low Self Worth*, York, Joseph Rowntree Foundation.

Katz, L. (1993) Distinction between self-esteem and narcissism: implications for practice, Eric/EECE, Archive of Publications and Resources, University of Illinois.

Self-esteem and individual differences

All people are different. Even amongst children in the same families there are differences. Children differ in their physical appearances, in their personalities, in their abilities, and in their interests. People can also differ in their ethnic group, their customs, their religions and in their race. These differences amongst people contribute to the rich tapestry of life. It would be a dull world if every person in it were the same.

Despite these observations, differences between people have often proved to be the sources of much tension in the world. From time immemorial, people have not always found individual differences easy to accept. It could be argued that the main problem facing humankind has always been how to get on with people who are different from us. The greater the difference the harder it seems to be to be able to get on with others. Whether people are able to live peaceably with one another seems to be largely a matter of degree of difference.

Teachers in the classroom should be aware of their own possible prejudices with regard to individual differences. We can all have a blind spot and we can all have times when we become victims of our culturally learned responses to individual differences. For instance, there is some research indicating that teachers tend to rate a child's personality as attractive simply because the child is physically attractive.

The same research shows how teachers tend to associate a child of attractive physical appearance as being of higher than average intellect. Continued judgements, made in this way, causing a teacher to react in a predetermined fashion towards a child, will affect their expectancies of that child. There will be a tendency for the child who is of attractive appearance to be expected to perform at a higher level than the child of lesser attractive appearance. This will affect the child's self-image and, with continued attention, would eventually affect their self-esteem.

■ ORIGINS OF DIFFERENCES ■

The relative roles of heredity and environment in creating individual differences are still being debated. Most authorities would agree that genetic factors have a role to play in individual differences and that environmental factors also have a role to play. It has not proved easy to disentangle the relative influences of heredity and environment. There is evidence that different socio-economic circumstances and different cultural values have a large part to play in differences of personality. Also, different family values and different child-rearing practices have a part to play. With regard to differences in intelligence, heredity appears to play the most significant role but, again, it is difficult to separate the affects of heredity from environmental factors.

■ CHILDREN'S REACTIONS TO INDIVIDUAL DIFFERENCES ■

Children are alike in many ways, but there are countless other ways in which children are different from each other. With the development of their self-image, children begin to be aware of their differences and are likely to react to them. This happens generally fairly soon after entry to nursery school.

This early stage is the time when children begin to form friendships. Children find comfort and security in discovering other children like themselves. The positive feedback each gives the other as a result of their mutual liking has an equally positive effect on their self-esteem. Children also discover some other children whom they almost instinctively dislike. They tend to avoid those they dislike and so will protect their self-esteem from possible negative comments. Many of the relationships formed at this time are transient, so a child may be an enemy on one day and a friend the next. Most childhood relationships at this stage are based on fairly superficial characteristics and specific social encounters. It would be rare at this time for children to react negatively to another child merely because they are different. Generally, negative emotional reactions based on prejudicial attitudes do not make their appearance until much later.

Where there are obvious differences between children, such as in physique, ethnicity or a severe disability, most children would react with interest. Only occasionally would a child react negatively and, if this does occur, it is likely to be the result of an attitude learned prior to entering school. As children progress through the school and their experiences are widened, they become increasingly subject to other outside influences. It is at that stage that some children begin to develop negative attitudes to other people who are different from themselves.

Some of the more frequent and varied individual physical, educational and social conditions that have the potential to affect children's self-esteem are listed below.

■ PHYSICAL DIFFERENCES ■

Children with a physical disability or a marked facial disfigurement will at some stage begin to be aware of being different from other children. With appropriate support many of these children will have the strength to cope with this, but some children will inevitably feel self-conscious and may become unduly anxious about the difference. There is an ample body of research to indicate that on meeting another person children and adults react first to their physical appearance. Body build appears to be an important factor in the process of early appraisal of others. Those who are either overweight or underweight tend to be viewed negatively as people. The evidence seems to suggest that although self-esteem is not in itself affected by a person's physical appearance, feedback from others certainly does.

As children develop, and particularly as they become influenced by the media, physical attractiveness becomes a major issue for many children, especially those at the adolescent stage. Moreover, it seems that this finding applies to both males and females.

Most children will accept another child who looks slightly different from themselves unless the difference is marked. Where one child has an obvious physical disability it is not easy for that child to be accepted without question. Most teachers would recognize this and deliberately set out to help the child who is very different adjust to the others in the class as well as helping the class adjust to the child involved. No matter how understanding the class, the child with the disability is bound to feel some degree of distress at being unlike the rest of the class. The teacher needs to be continually aware of the child's progress in adjusting to the group. If allowed to fall by the wayside, low self-esteem soon sets in.

■ SPECIFIC LEARNING DIFFICULTIES■

Children with specific learning difficulties are at risk of developing low self-esteem unless it is recognized and they receive appropriate help. One of the most frequently encountered specific learning difficulties is dyslexia. It has become a vast topic for research in recent years and it is not intended here to discuss this concept in any detail. However, the child with dyslexia is especially at risk of developing low self-esteem and, as it seems that at least 4 per cent of the school population has dyslexia, it is important to include some discussion of this.

At the time of writing this book there is no international consensus on a definition of dyslexia. However, most research workers would agree that it is a specific learning difficulty centred mainly on the development of language skills. The dyslexic child is often highly intelligent but is rarely able to demonstrate their level of intellect owing to their language difficulties. They are likely to be slow to read and to learn to spell accurately, as well as having other possible difficulties associated with working memory.

An early identification of dyslexia can prevent serious frustrations for the child. With appropriate remedial help that also includes them being allowed extra time to complete work, the risk of developing low self-esteem for the dyslexic child is minimized. However, the fact is that there is no generally accepted early screening programme for these children, so many dyslexic children remain unidentified. Consequently, their learning difficulties are undiagnosed and they are often in doubt about their intelligence. Left in this situation, before long, they develop low self-esteem.

Self-esteem enhancement programmes and activities would most certainly be of considerable value to dyslexic children. Their sources of frustration would be able to be expressed safely within the trusting atmosphere of a typical session. However, they may not always be able to respond as well as the other children during the activities. Where a child is known to have been identified with dyslexia, the teacher should always be ready to allow that child extra time to complete any written activity. Additionally, it is not uncommon for the dyslexic child to be slow to respond orally as accurate word retrieval can be a problem. Again, a teacher who is aware of the child's condition can assist that child by allowing more time for the child to respond otherwise the child may begin to feel inadequate.

There is another frequently occurring type of specific learning difficulty that is often not easy to identify. This is known as *scotopic sensitivity*. It seems that some children can be sensitive to different light frequencies so that they quickly become fatigued after prolonged written work or reading. Words often become blurred for these children. Children with scotopic sensitivity may also have some difficulty with visual tracking when reading. As a result, when reading they have a tendency to underline each sentence with their fingers. Unless this problem is recognized and verified early, the child may try to avoid reading and so incur the disapproval of the teacher. With regular disapproval would come resentment so that eventually the child would develop low self-esteem.

■ HEARING DIFFICULTIES ■

The emotional and social effects of a hearing loss are well documented in the literature. Children with a hearing loss are at risk of developing low self-esteem as so much of communication is oral. These children are well aware that their speech is not always being understood. Also, there may be a tendency for other children to become irritated with their occasional lack of verbal response.

A hearing loss is a 'hidden disability'. It cannot be observed directly as with a physical disability. Consequently, the child with a hearing loss can easily be misunderstood. This can lead to intense frustration and result in a range of defensive reactions ranging from withdrawal to aggressive behaviour. However the child reacts to the frustration, the child with a hearing loss may experience negative reactions from the other children. If this continues, they will begin to perceive themselves as unpopular so that eventually this will lead to low self-esteem. With understanding and sympathy none of these problems need occur. However, it is clear that a child with a hearing loss is usually at risk of developing low self-esteem.

> SYMPATHY. This is often contrasted with empathy and refers to the ability to sympathize with another person's distress but without necessarily experiencing it.

■VISUAL DIFFICULTIES■

The effects of a visual impairment are just as well documented in the literature as those with a hearing loss. Most children with a visual disability will have been identified before their entry into school. Children who have a severe visual impairment are usually placed in a special school, while those with lesser impairment are increasingly being integrated in the main school system. Again, a child with visual difficulties is usually at more risk than the other children of developing low self-esteem. Even with sympathetic understanding from the other children they often feel isolated, as they are not always able to participate in the same physical activities as the rest of the class.

■GENERAL LEARNING DIFFICULTY■

The phrase 'general learning difficulty' is used to describe children who have a difficulty learning and retaining new material. They are usually slow to learn and can often appear to be unmotivated. They usually score well below average on tests of intelligence. As with most disabilities, provided they receive sympathetic handling and are allowed to work at their own pace there need not be a problem. However, there is some research demonstrating a correlation between IQ and self-esteem. Where a child with a general learning difficulty is placed in a class alongside another child of average or above average ability then the first child will almost inevitably feel inadequate. This raises the topic of whether to integrate or to segregate children with general learning difficulties. This issue has been a topic of debate in education for many decades and the arguments continue.

Depending, of course, on the degree of learning difficulty, a child with a general learning difficulty is usually aware of their differences from other children and so may begin to feel inadequate. This can be exacerbated if he/she has to compete and to socialize with other brighter children. With regard to the effects on the self-esteem of a child, it seems that the particular organization in a school does not matter so much as the quality of the relationship that exists between the teacher and the child in that particular school.

■ GENDER DIFFERENCES ■

It is an inescapable fact that sex stereotyping begins at an early age and long before children begin school. Rigid cultural stereotyping may not be as common as it used to be but it continues to operate to some degree in most families. Boys are still, on the whole, expected to be 'tougher' than girls and are usually given more mechanical toys to play with than girls. Girls are encouraged to be caring and motherly, and would usually be given more dolls than boys.

However, sex stereotyping is not restricted to parental influences. Teachers are also products of their social group and have predetermined attitudes. Amongst these attitudes, and possible prejudices, they have expectancies regarding sex roles. Their particular expectancies will reinforce children's self-concepts accordingly.

Further dilemmas are now occurring regarding some children who display same-sex sexuality. Teachers of older children and adolescents may need to address the gender dilemmas facing gay and lesbian children and their families. In previous decades same-sex sexuality was pathologized. However, contemporary initiatives now include whole school initiatives to lessen anti-homosexual prejudice and to encourage peer support and greater social acceptance of all children (Crowley *et al.*, 2001). The review of the literature indicates that there is more risk of gay and lesbian people attempting self-harm and suicide than amongst the heterosexual population (Warwick *et al.*, 2000). This suggests a possible correlation between homosexual children and low self-esteem.

The influence of heredity on male–female differences is conflicting but it would seem that males are genetically programmed to be more assertive than girls, although there are exceptions to this. There are also biological differences such as greater muscular development in boys that tend to point boys in the direction of more physical pursuits. When children first enter school a the primary stage it seems that they generally choose their friends not on the basis of their sex but on their interests and overall attractiveness. It is only as puberty begins to appear that children tend more to choose to remain within their own sex for their friendships. Social pressures point the sexes in different directions. To expect children of the opposite sex to play and work together regularly at this stage can produce problems for some of them.

Whilst there are no doubt physiological differences between the sexes, it is not possible to disentangle the relative influences of heredity and culture when explaining these differences. From the point of view of self-esteem development, the teacher in the classroom needs continually to be aware of these differences and the observation that boys and girls often derive their self-esteem from different sources. Boys in general derive their self-esteem more from achievements while girls tend to derive theirs more from social competence. This difference between the sexes becomes more exaggerated as the child develops.

■ DIFFERENT ETHNIC GROUPS ■

Schools in the United Kingdom are usually multiracial with varying proportions of children from different ethnic groups. Some immigrant families tend to choose to locate to areas where others from their original country are already living. This is understandable. It means that some schools, in the inter-city areas particularly, have a larger proportion of children from different ethnic groups. Consequently, the children in these schools do not have the opportunity to learn the customs and mores of the predominant culture. Conversely, children from the predominant culture have no opportunity to learn others' customs. This lack of understanding can cause friction when the different cultures eventually meet outside school.

With regard to the development of self-esteem, there is some evidence that children in a minority ethnic group tend to have lower self-esteem than other children in the same school (Burns, 1982). This is largely due to the insecurity they experience when having to accept social values different from their own and having to face racial prejudice. The teacher would need to be aware of these potential sources of friction. Some of the activities outlined in Chapter 8 designed to help children respect cultural differences might usefully be applied if this situation occurs.

■ FURTHER READING■

Burns, R. (1982) *Self-Concept Development and Education*, London, Holt Rinehart & Winston.

Crowley, C., Hallam, S., Harre, R. and Lunt, I. (2001) Study support for young people with same-sex attraction: views and experiences from a pioneering peer support initiative in the north of England, *Educational and Child Psychology*, Vol 18, no. 1, pp. 108–24.

Jenks, C. (1996) *Childhood*, London, Routledge.

Roffey, S., Tarrant, T. and Majors, K. (1994) *Young Friends: Schools and Friendships*, London, Cassell.

Warwick, I., Oliver, C. and Aggleton, P. (2000) Sexuality and mental health promotion: lesbian and gay young people, in P. Aggleton, J. Hurry and I. Warwick (eds), *Young People and Mental Health*, Chichester, Wiley.

4

Significant influences on the self-concept

Most children will have countless learning experiences before they begin school, so they will arrive at school already with a rudimentary self-concept. Some children will enter school already with low self-esteem. There will be others who will be confident and have a high self-esteem, while most will probably have moderately high self-esteem. It is useful for teachers to be aware of the various influences that have formed the current level of a child's self-esteem before they enter school.

■ PARENTAL INFLUENCES ■

Young children are wholly dependent at first on the family group for their general well-being. This includes their self-esteem development. Very soon after entering the world the newborn baby probably develops an impression of whether their environment is satisfying or otherwise. At this stage, they still have no sense of personal identity or self-image. During these early months, the child is learning a sense of whether to trust others or to be wary of them. A particular family's child-rearing practices gradually begin to have an effect on the child's self-concept. Whilst most parents love their children and this will be communicated to their children, there are some children who right from the beginning learn that life is often a hostile place and that they themselves are not very lovable. These are the children who probably arrive at school with low self-esteem. There are various degrees of low self-esteem depending not only on the child's early experiences in the family, but also on the constitutional make up of the child.

The personality of a child is determined by the interaction of heredity and environment. Although early environmental influences undoubtedly have an effect, the constitutional make-up of the child ultimately determines the effects of this early treatment. Children are born with varying degrees of strength, not only physically but also in personality. Some parents make the mistake of thinking that their influence on the child is paramount. For instance, many parents have blamed themselves for their child's difficult behaviour when it has been the constitutional make-up of the child that has been responsible for the behaviour. It is extremely difficult to separate the effects of heredity and environment when considering the origins of individual differences.

There have been several monumental studies over the years on the significance of different parental child-rearing practices on children's self-esteem (Bowlby, 1951; Rosenburg, 1965; Coopersmith, 1967). They all conclude that democratic child-rearing practices, the establishment of warm relationships, the setting of limits to behaviour and the self-esteem of the mother are all conducive to high self-esteem in children. The opposite of these qualities – authoritarian attitudes, permissiveness, indifference, hostility and low self-esteem of the mother – have been seen to result in low self-esteem in the child. It is interesting that most studies demonstrate that the mother's influence is a more significant factor in the early development of a child's self-esteem than their father's influence.

It is generally accepted that almost from birth parents will socialize their children mainly in terms of their sex roles. As children develop, sex stereotyping continues to be reinforced. For instance, boys are more likely to be given mechanical toys as presents whilst girls will be more likely to be given dolls. With further development, boys tend to identify mainly with the father and imitate his behaviour, whilst girls will tend to identify with the mother and imitate her behaviour.

CHANGES IN FAMILY STRUCTURE

Divorces, bereavements, separations, and family relocations, usually result in changes in a family's lifestyle. All these events that may occur in children's lives have the potential to affect their self-concepts. There will be the inevitable emotional trauma associated with these major events. In addition, there are often environmental changes compounding a child's emotional distress. A change of employment by the family breadwinner sometimes necessitates a family relocation to a new neighbourhood. This usually means also a change of school. Previous friendships are left behind and there is the need to form new ones. There can also be financial worries arising from sudden parental unemployment that can result in the lowering of a family's standard of living.

Whilst in general there does not appear to be a correlation between socio-economic factors and self-esteem in children, a sudden change of circumstances may result in temporary emotional upheavals. Paradoxically, there are specific geographic areas where poverty and social disadvantage have had a negative effect on a family's aspirations leaving children unmotivated and ill prepared for school attendance. Whilst poverty in itself does not constitute a negative outcome for the development of positive self-esteem, a cluster of negative factors are known to combine to create areas of social deprivation (MacKay and Watson, 1999). Currently, the government in the United Kingdom has recognized these areas of need and has established initiatives with appropriate funding for early intervention programmes to counteract the effects of social deprivation (DfES, 2003; 2004).

Whatever changes occur in a family's circumstances or its structure, it is the way that the whole family reacts to the changes, the emotional support they give one another and their expectancies for the future that are the prime influences on the child's developing self-concept. However, these are not the only influences.

PEER AND SIBLING INFLUENCES

Once a child has learned to verbalize and has developed some independence of movement, the influences of siblings and peers appear to be significant factors in the continued formation of their self-esteem. During school years, peers and siblings are often a more significant source of a child's self-esteem than their own parents.

However, whereas in the family it is the behaviour of the child that mediates the child's self-esteem, interaction with siblings and peers focuses more on performance. This observation reflects the emergence of the child's specific areas of self-esteem as opposed to the development of the child's global self-esteem. Once the child enters the playground, specific influences such as physical performance become important sources of self-esteem. In the classroom, it is usually academic performance that is valued more. These factors may have been minimized in the family but in the school environment they suddenly become significant. It is difficult for a child to maintain self-esteem if he/she is physically incompetent on the sports field or demonstrates learning difficulties in the classroom.

Friendships become a significant source of self-esteem as the child receives feedback from them. Although children in primary school usually place value on social relationships for their own sake, a child's popularity in school, and ultimately their self-esteem, is often determined equally by their performance in other spheres of activity. This contrasts with the main source of their self-esteem in the family, where it is the child's behaviour and the attitude of the parents towards this behaviour that are usually the more significant factors.

As children develop and their social environment is expanded, they encounter many more activities and develop many more interests in common with their peers. These new areas of interest and experience might include, for example, music, special crafts or sports, all of which present the children with opportunities to compare themselves with their peers. It seems that children at this age are competitive and it becomes important to them that they excel in their newly found pursuits. Successes and failures in these endeavours have varying impacts on the children's specific self-esteem. Whether their successes or their failures ultimately affect their global self-esteem will depend on the particular value placed by their group on their performance. Failure on the sports field for instance will not affect global self-esteem if the particular school places more value on academic performance. In this example, neither would success on the sports field affect global self-esteem.

■FAILURE EXPERIENCES■

There has been some recent discussion on the desirability of omitting the word 'failure' from a teacher's estimate of a child's performance. This view is an example of how self-esteem enhancement is often misunderstood. It could be argued that failure is inevitable in life. There will always be somebody who is more competent at all activities and in all areas of life, and only one person at any one time can be at the top. It is not failure that is the problem. It is the attitudes towards failure that can lower self-esteem. Also, there is evidence for the value of trial-end-error learning, where children learn from making mistakes and from failing. Whether a child will be affected by failure is dependent not only on the criticisms of others, but also on their own self-evaluation.

Where children are consistently criticized and attacked for not achieving standards demanded by others, then low self-esteem will follow. If the same children are encouraged and praised for their efforts, despite not having achieved these expected standards, their self-esteem is more likely to be maintained. Moreover, these children will be more likely also to try again to achieve the expected standards. This philosophy would apply to both performance and behaviour, and assumes that the standards in question are reasonable.

It is interesting that where children already have high self-esteem they will not be so easily influenced or feel threatened by negative criticism from others. So, for instance, if criticized for not behaving appropriately or for not having succeeded in a specific task, they are more likely to accept the criticism objectively without becoming personally upset. They are likely to develop the attitude of wishing to improve next time. The probable reason why the high self-esteem child is less easily upset by criticism is that one characteristic of high self-esteem is the ability to be self-determinate.

Another factor involved in whether a child will be negatively affected by criticism following failure is the credibility and status of the person who does the criticizing. Teachers and parents are in a powerful position in this respect. However, as the child reaches adolescence teachers' and parents' influence recedes to some degree. Peers become a major source of self-esteem, as does the media.

■ MEDIA INFLUENCES ■

There is no doubt about the role played by television, radio, music, films, books and magazines in the formation of public taste. A more recent addition to this list has been the Internet. Adolescents are particularly influenced by what they see and hear in the media. The typical adolescent is seeking an identity and so is ready to identify with imagined heroes.

Whilst most of the media probably reflects the cultural values of the group to which the child belongs, this cannot always be applied. This is manifested particularly in the influence of the Internet where negative values and standards can so easily be promulgated. It seems that the time spent on the Internet by a child can be a source of conflict with his/her parents. Firm, but understanding, parental control is essential in these circumstances if the self-esteem of the child is to be preserved.

Even where the influences of the media are relatively benevolent, parents still need to be aware of their effect on their children. There is some concern over the fact that many children are spending more time in front of a television or a computer screen than with their parents or outside with their peers. This minimizing of social interaction can only have a negative effect on the child's social development and, ultimately, on the child's self-concept.

Even if programmes on television do not necessarily consist of undesirable material, they may still have an undesirable effect on children. For instance, popular programmes such as soap operas, are renowned for reinforcing traditional sex-stereotyping. Men are often portrayed as more aggressive and more outgoing than women, who are presented as more caring and less aggressive.

Whilst undoubtedly there are some individuals who present themselves in this stereotypical way, the stereotyping of the sexes in real life is not as common a phenomenon today. Society has changed and continues to do so with regard to sex roles. It is not uncommon, for instance, to find a father at home caring full-time for the child whilst the mother goes out to work.

■ ADOLESCENCE ■

In some societies adolescence is marked by an initiation ceremony. This leaves the person in no doubt that they have now left childhood behind and entered the adult world. There are no such definitive ceremonies in our Western society and the passage from childhood to adulthood is an ambiguous time for adolescents. This can produce all kinds of insecurities and threats to self-esteem in adolescent children.

Children in Western society are often unsure of their roles and of what behaviour is expected from them. This insecurity and search for identity, combined with the hormonal pressures of puberty, often contribute to the renowned problems associated with adolescence. The young child's self-image is largely taken from identification with the parents. Their ideal self is also a product of the parents' values and standards. In adolescence the balance changes as the values and standards of the peer group and the media all impinge on the young adult's search for identity.

Adolescence is a period of experimentation and exploration as different identities and different attitudes are tried. Central to this time of rapid change is the adolescent's relationship to authority. Their need to be independent unfortunately conflicts with their continued reliance on their family for economic and safety needs. On the one hand they are protesting independence, whilst on the other they continue to need the security of the family. This conflict is the root of much of the adolescent's rebellious stage.

The adolescent's challenging behaviour is often accompanied by swings of emotion so that one minute they hate everybody and the next minute they love them. This behaviour makes the adolescent more vulnerable to outside influences, with the attendant risk of developing low self-esteem. Many parents have said that they no longer recognize their child at this stage and fear that they have lost them. Wise parents and wise teachers will recognize this as a temporary stage of development and will not overreact to what often appears to be deliberate rudeness and emotional overreaction.

Cognitive development shows a surge in the adolescent that can be seen in their sudden interest in politics and the wider issues in society. However, their new-found intellectual interests can once again place them at risk of developing low self-esteem. This is because their relative emotional immaturity often results in negative criticism as they tend to overstate their case. Once again, it is often wiser to accept their viewpoint without demolishing it.

Body image is a major source of identity for children at all ages but in adolescence it begins to assume a central role with regard to the development of their self-image. Reinforced by advertising and the media generally, adolescents suddenly become very aware of their physical appearance. Boys suddenly care about their hair. This can cause parental amusement where for many years they may have had conflicts over washing it. Girls who previously may have lacked dress sense suddenly become fashion-conscious and have to have the latest fashionable clothes. This difference between the sexes becomes more marked at this stage than in previous years.

There is some evidence that, with regard to the development of self-esteem, adolescent boys are more concerned that they are seen to be athletic and muscular whilst girls are more concerned that they have an attractive face, hair, bust, teeth and mouth. The physical attributes that constitute attractiveness at this stage for both sexes are determined mainly by the media and advertising. Clearly, dissatisfaction with physical appearance can be a source of low self-esteem for boys and girls.

The ambiguities of their identity, their challenges with authority and the general emotional upheavals of this stage are likely to be the main reasons for adolescents' need to belong to their own group. So it is that adolescence is a time when they tend to gather together in coffee bars or similar establishments where they can feel secure amongst their own kind. The family is no longer their total source of security. Parental values are often rejected. The values of their gang have more influence in determining their values at this stage. Once again, the wise parent and teacher will recognize this as only a stage.

The loss of one's identity is a well-known symptom of mental illness. The adolescent who is seeking an identity is not mentally ill but for some adolescents, their search for an identity could, in one sense, be regarded as a temporary mild form of illness. Those who have had an emotionally satisfying early childhood with loving parents do not seem to be quite so badly affected by this identity crisis. For those who have not had the good fortune of a confident start in life the insecurities of not knowing precisely who they are can be extremely disturbing. It is not surprising, therefore, that some adolescents appear mistrustful and full of anxieties, with corresponding low self-esteem.

■ CULTURAL IDENTITY ■

Children begin by identifying with their family group and, as they develop, most of them extend their group allegiance to incorporate the neighbourhood group, their school, their religion and, eventually, their country. If asked, most children would be able to declare their religion and their nationality. All these experiences form part of their developing self-image. The identification with particular groups also gives a secure feeling of belonging that contributes to the development of high self-esteem.

For some children, living in Britain can lead to an increased interest in their own traditional values and so reinforce their identity with their families' cultural patterns (Lau, 2000). Although generally belonging to a group is a positive experience, it can sometimes be a negative one. For instance, in a multicultural society the identification with a particular nationality sometimes can produce insecurities for children when they encounter different cultural values. Most children have no problem in relating to children from different nationalities and many rejoice in the differences that they find interesting. However, some new immigrants to a country can find it difficult to relinquish the cultural values and practices of their old country. If these values conflict with the cultural values of their new country, their children can find themselves in an ambiguous situation. This can be an even bigger problem where the child happens to be born in the new country. Their parents' cultural values may be totally foreign to them and this can produce conflicts within the family. These children feel unable to identify completely with either culture and that has the potential for causing low self-esteem.

Families differ in the emphasis they place on belonging to a religious group and some have no allegiance to a particular religion. However, there are potential conflicts for children when they come into contact with the values of religious groups that may be different from their own. Most schools have a particular religious orientation and usually present a fair spectrum of other different religions. It is important for the child's developing self-esteem that their particular religion is given respect, and teachers have an important role in ensuring this.

■OTHER CRISES■

Children are sometimes victims of various traumatic events outside school or witness such events. Amongst these possible events are road traffic accidents, bereavements, criminal assaults and natural disasters including floods and fires. Also, an increasing number of children are arriving in schools as war refugees from other countries.

Any one of these disturbing events can affect the whole school, leaving children traumatized and in need of emotional support and counselling (Yule and Gold, 1993). Without parental support and mechanisms within the school itself these events can have a long-term negative effect on the child's developing self-concept.

In conclusion, there are a multitude of experiences that begin to form a child's self-concept. The significant people in the child's life at any one time have the greatest influence on their self-concept. The family initially has the greatest influence but this gradually gives way to other groups in the child's experiences, including the school, the neighbourhood and, eventually, the nation.

It might be thought that the teacher's influence on the child's self-esteem would be minimal in the light of so many other possible influences in the life of that child. However, as the author's research reported in this book (see Appendix) demonstrates, the teacher is potentially in a position to have a powerful influence on the child's self-esteem. Whether this happens depends largely on the personal qualities of the teacher and the kind of relationships established with children. This topic is pursued further in Chapter 6.

■FURTHER READING■

Buckingham, D. (2000) *After the Death of Childhood: Growing up in the Age of Electronic Media*, Oxford, Blackwell Priory.

Department for Education and Skills (DfES) (2003) *Every Child Matters*, London, The Stationery Office.

Department for Education and Skills (DfES) (2004) *Every Child Matters: Next Steps*, London, The Stationery Office.

Giddens, A. (1991) *Modernity and Self-identity: Self and Society in the Late Modern Age*, Cambridge, Polity.

Lau, A. (ed.) (2000) *South Asian Children and Adolescents in Britain*, London, Whurr.

Lawrence, A. (2004) *Principles of Child Protection: Management and Practice*, Maidenhead, McGraw-Hill.

MacKay, T. and Watson, K. (1999) Literacy social disadvantage and early intervention: enhancing reading achievement in primary school, *Educational and Child Psychology*, Vol. 16, no. 1, pp. 30–6.

Troyna, B. and Hatcher, R. (1992) *Racism in Children's Lives: A Study of Mainly White Primary Schools*, London, Routledge.

Young, L. and Bagley, C. (1982) Self esteem, self concept and the development of black identity: a theoretical overview, in G. Verma and C. Bagley (eds), *Self Concept, Achievement and Multicultural Education*, London, Macmillan.

Yule, W. and Gold, A. (1993) *Wise Before the Event: Coping with Crises in Schools*, London, Calouste Gulbenkian Foundation.

Assessing self-esteem

■ MEASURING SELF-ESTEEM ■

No area of psychological research is currently more popular or more confused than that having to do with the measurement of the self-concept. (Combs et al., 1963)

The above statement was made over 40 years ago and the situation has changed very little since then. There are now hundreds of articles and books on enhancing self-esteem, and they contain almost as many different ways of measuring the concept. Perhaps, it is not surprising to find so many different methods of measuring self-esteem when for many years there was no consensus on the definition of self-esteem.

In theory it should be a simple matter to identify those with low self-esteem. Having defined self-esteem as 'the individual's affective evaluation of the discrepancy between self-image and ideal self', surely, it might be argued, all that is required is to devise a series of questions which ask the individual how he/she feels about this discrepancy. Where such measures have been devised, very few methods of assessing self-esteem can be considered to be reliable and valid for the purpose of practical usage in the classroom. Reference to the history of the research into self-concept explains the reasons for this.

Just as there have been so many different theories of personality over the years, inevitably there have been many different definitions of self-esteem and, as a result, many different kinds of assessment procedures (Wylie, 1974). In a book such as this, one that aims to be a practical book, a review of the methodology would be inappropriate. It is appropriate, however, that teachers are aware of some of the difficulties involved in accurately assessing self-esteem. The main difficulties involved in measuring self-esteem are discussed below.

First, the teacher has to decide which aspect of self-esteem requires measuring. Is it global self-esteem or situation-specific self-esteem? The reader will recall that global self-esteem refers to an overall feeling of worth, whilst specific self-esteem refers to numerous spheres of activity each of which can have a different measure. Children often evaluate themselves differently in different areas of their lives. Amongst these different situation-specific self-esteems could be the child's academic self-esteem, their physical self-esteem, their social self-esteem or their sporting self-esteem. It is not unusual for children to feel differently about each of these different areas of their lives.

Having decided what it is that the teacher wishes to measure, they should then take a cautious attitude when choosing a particular method of measurement as there can be many pitfalls along the way. Foremost amongst the pitfalls, for the unwary, is the nature of self-esteem assessment itself.

It is important to acknowledge that self-esteem cannot be observed directly but has to be inferred. A child's self-esteem can be inferred either from a self-report or from observation by the teacher. Both methods have their limitations.

The first possible difficulty with the self-report method is the lack of awareness of self that some children possess. Many young children are often relatively unconscious of themselves. For them any measure of self-esteem is likely to produce unreliable results. A reflection on their self-esteem can be far too sophisticated an exercise for some children. This is perhaps not surprising, considering that one process of development is that of becoming more aware of self. This may not be quite such a problem with older children. Having said that, even some adults lack this awareness or insight into themselves. The next possible pitfall is the language used in some questionnaires and rating scales. Words can mean different things to different people and the words may not be in a particular child's vocabulary. A thorough knowledge of the children being assessed usually surmounts this difficulty.

Perhaps a more common pitfall is what is known as the 'social expectancy, social desirability syndrome'. This means that some children may report their feelings in terms of what they believe their teacher expects. For instance, if the relationship with the teacher is a good one they will know that the teacher wants them to be happy, so if asked whether they are happy they will inevitably say 'yes' no matter what may be their true feelings. This is more likely to be a problem when assessing younger children, although many older children can also be subjected to this phenomenon.

A common way of coping with low-self-esteem, particulary amongst older children, is to develop what are known as 'ego defense mechanisms'. As they do not wish to accept a specific inadequacy they will look for a face-saving reason for it, and so may not give an honest reply to a questionnaire. This is a problem with all personality questionnaires and not just with self-esteem measures.

Children can manifest radically different behaviour as a response to their low self-esteem. As mentioned in Chapter 1, people's personality can be found to lie somewhere along the continuum of introversion/extroversion. It seems to be the case that those with problems tend to be at the extremes of this continuum. Therefore, it is possible broadly to group the low self-esteem children into those whose reaction is introverted and those whose reaction to low self-esteem is more extroverted.

From the work of Eysenck (1980) it seems that people react to frustration in terms of their basic personality type. The markedly introverted child will appear relatively apathetic, whereas the markedly extroverted child will perhaps appear as boastful and arrogant. Both these types of behaviour could be interpreted as examples of 'ego defense mechanisms'. In the latter case, it is likely to be a compensation for feelings of inferiority. Inevitably in both these examples, responses to being asked a sensitive question will tend to be less than honest.

Finally, there is the question of the reliability and validity of the measuring instrument. A good measure will be reliable, meaning that the same result would be obtained if the measure was readministered shortly after its first administration. There are degrees of reliability and an applied statistical technique will give a reliability figure. All published measures should include this figure in a handbook accompanying the instrument. The degree of validity is the extent to which the measure is really assessing what it sets out to assess. For instance, some questionnaires, particularly if administered to young children, may be a test of their vocabulary rather than their self-esteem. The validity of a measure should also be listed in the handbook.

No measure of self-esteem is perfect and there are many limitations to all of them. There are often the statistical limitations of the measuring instrument itself as well as the limitations of the child being assessed. However, provided that the teacher is aware of these limitations, and the possible pitfalls, there are several measuring instruments that could be usefully employed in measuring of children's self-esteem. Some of these are discussed below.

■ BEHAVIOURAL CHECKLIST ■

The teacher acquainted with self-concept theory as outlined in Chapter 1 will be on the lookout for the child who lacks confidence, who seems apathetic, who seems unable to take risks and the like. Indeed, the following behavioural checklist might be used to assess low self-esteem:

- Does he/she make self-disparaging remarks?
- Is he/she boastful?
- Is he/she hesitant and timid in new situations?
- Does he/she make excuses to avoid situations which may be stressful?
- Is he/she continually asking for help and/or reassurance?
- Is he/she continually asking if he/she is liked or is popular?

- Does he/she hang back and remain on the fringe of a group?

- Is he/she apathetic in a learning situation?

- Does he/she daydream a lot?

- Does he/she avoid work even though risking your displeasure?

- Does he/she tend to blame others for his/her failures?

- Is he/she reluctant to assume responsibilities?

The checklist method is probably the simplest to use and is useful as long as we remember its limitations.

■ THE LAWRENCE SELF-ESTEEM QUESTIONNAIRE (THE LAWSEQ)■

The questionnaire method is also useful provided that the standardization has been thorough and that good rapport is established between teacher and children before it is administered. Teachers may find the Lawseq useful owing to its brevity and its high reliability and validity. The Lawseq is a particularly well standardized questionnaire and was selected for use in the 1979 National Child Development Study when it was administered to 15,000 boys and girls of primary age. Full details of the standardization are given in Lawrence (1982; 1983). The Lawseq questionnaire is shown with the primary school version in Figure 2.1 and the secondary school version in Figure 2.2.

There are many factors that can affect the reliability of a test when measuring self-esteem. When using the Lawseq questionnaire the quality of the rapport established between tester and child is crucial in ensuring its reliability. The chances of a child being willing to confide intimate feelings are considerably reduced unless there is rapport with the tester.

The teacher should establish rapport with the child prior to administering the Lawseq. The particular format of establishing this relationship will depend on two factors. The first consideration is the age of the child being tested. The words used with a primary age child will be different from the words used with a secondary age child. The second consideration is whether it is intended to assess self-esteem in a group situation or with an individual child.

The following different formats are suggested according to the different circumstances listed above.

GROUP TESTING

- (Primary and secondary) Ensure the group is relaxed and attentive.

- (Primary age) Teacher introduces the session with 'I am interested in knowing how happy you are in school. It would help me to know this if you answered some questions on this paper I'm going to give you'. (Shows the questionnaire).

- (Secondary age) 'I am interested in ensuring that you all enjoy school. So I would be glad if you would help me with this by answering a questionnaire.'

- (Primary and secondary) 'Before I give out the questions I have to tell you that this is not a test. There are no wrong answers. All answers will be correct ones'.

- (Primary) 'I also want to tell you that your answers will be a secret. Nobody but me will know what you have written'.

- (Secondary) 'As all the answers will be kept confidential so please do not look at your neighbour's answers. Nobody but me will know what you have written.'

- (Primary and secondary) Teacher gives out the questionnaires. Once each child has a copy, teacher says 'You will see next to each question a space to tick Yes, No, or Don't know'. Teacher writes this on the blackboard and shows the group how to record their answers.

- (Primary and secondary) Teacher instructs the group to tick Don't know if they are unsure how to respond saying 'Children often find it hard to know what to answer so don't worry if you have to tick Don't know'.

- Teacher reads out each question in turn allowing 2 minutes between each. Child has the questionnaire and follows each question silently as teacher reads aloud.

- (Secondary) Completion of the questionnaire might be an opportunity for the teacher to introduce the topic of self-esteem for discussion.

LAWSEQ
PRIMARY SCHOOL VERSION

Yes   No   Don't
know

1. Do you think that your parents usually like to hear about your ideas?
2. Do you often feel lonely at school?
3. Do other children often break friends or fall out with you?
4. Do you like team games?
5. Do you think that other children often say nasty things about you?
6. When you have to say things in front of teachers, do you usually feel shy?
7. Do you like writing stories or doing creative writing?
8. Do you often feel sad because you have nobody to play with at school?
9. Are you good at mathematics?
10. Are there lots of things about yourself you would like to change?
11. When you have to say things in front of other children, do you usually feel foolish?
12. Do you find it difficult to do things like woodwork or knitting?
13. When you want to tell a teacher something do you usually feel foolish?
14 Do you often have to find new friends because your old friends are playing with somebody else?
15. Do you usually feel foolish when you talk to your parents?
16. Do other people often think that you tell lies?

KEY:

Score +2 for all numbers answering 'no' *except* for question 1. Score +2 for question 1 answering 'yes'. 4, 7, 9, 12 do not count.

Score +1 for all answers 'don't know'.

© 1996 Denis Lawrence

Figure 2.1 *Lawseq pupil questionnaire: primary school version*

LAWSEQ
SECONDARY SCHOOL VERSION

Yes   No   Don't
know

1. Do you think that your parents usually like to hear about your ideas?
2. Do you often feel lonely at school?
3. Do other students often get fed up with you and stop being friends with you?
4. Do you like outdoor games?
5. Do you think that other students often dislike you?
6. When you have to say things in front of teachers, do you usually feel shy?
7. Do you like writing stories or doing creative writing?
8 Do you often feel sad because you have nobody to talk to at school?
9. Are you good at mathematics?
10. Are there lots of things about yourself you would like to change?
11. When you have to say things in front of other students, do you usually feel foolish?
12. Do you find it difficult to do things like woodwork or knitting?
13. When you want to tell a teacher something do you usually feel foolish?
14. Do you often have to find new friends because your old friends prefer others to you?
15. Do you usually feel foolish when you talk to your parents?
16. Do other people often think that you tell lies?

KEY:

Score +2 for all numbers answering 'no' *except* for question 1. Score +2 for question 1 answering 'yes'. 4, 7, 9, 12 do not count.

Score +1 for all answers 'don't know'.

© 1996 Denis Lawrence

Figure 2.2 *Lawseq pupil questionnaire: secondary school version*

INDIVIDUAL TESTING

■ (Primary and secondary) Ask the child in advance of the session if they would like to have a chat about how they are settling in at school. Arrange a day and time, informing the child that it would only be for a few minutes.

■ (Primary) 'Thank you for coming. I like to know that the children are happy in school so I thought I would see some of them by themselves and it is your turn today.'

■ (Secondary) 'Thank you for coming. I like to be sure that all children in my class are enjoying school so I am seeing some of you individually for this purpose.'

■ (Primary) 'To help me know how best to make you happy in school I need to know more about you. Would you help me to do that by answering the questions I have on this paper?' Teacher then gives reassurances over confidentiality, as in the group test situation above.

■ (Secondary) 'I need to know how you feel about yourself so I can ensure that you enjoy school. Would you like to help me by filling in this questionnaire?' Teacher explains the questionnaire recording procedure and asks if the child would prefer the teacher to read out the questionnaire or whether they would prefer to fill it in themselves. Teacher then gives reassurance over confidentiality as in the group test situation above.

■ (Primary and secondary) On completion of the questionnaire the child should be thanked for helping and congratulated for having done the task. 'Thank you for helping! You've done that really well!'

Both of these questionnaires have been standardized on an English and an Australian population with the following norms:

Primary version	Mean = 19 SD = 4
Secondary school version	Mean = 18 SD = 4

The relevant questionnaire provides a useful screening device for the busy teacher new to a class and who would like to make a quick assessment. It also provides the teacher with a handy research tool for those who may be embarking on a self-esteem enhancement programme and require a 'before' and 'after' measure.

The Lawseq would seem to be the teacher's favoured method of assessing self-esteem in children to date.

■ OTHER METHODS OF ASSESSMENT■

Bearing in mind some of the major difficulties of assessment referred to earlier, there are other methods of assessment which the teacher may wish to consider in particular circumstances.

RATING SCALES

Rating scales are useful when the teacher may be interested in assessing perhaps only one or two aspects of self-esteem, for example, reluctance to attempt a new task. A 3- or 5-point scale could be used and the pupil rated accordingly:

'Afraid to attempt a new task'
Always – Sometimes – Never

ADJECTIVAL DISCREPANCIES

Adjectival discrepancies constitute a method of assessing the relationship between two different attitudes and were used by James (1890) who devised the formula:

Self-esteem = Success + Pretensions

The modern form of this equation has been used by presenting a list of predetermined adjectives. The respondent is asked to go through the list; the first time a tick is placed against those adjectives which *apply* to themselves and the second time a tick is placed next to those adjectives which the person *would like to apply* to themselves. The total discrepancy between the two scores is then the measure of self-esteem.

SEMANTIC DIFFERENTIAL

Semantic differential is a variation of the adjectival discrepancy method but this time each adjective is paired with its opposite, for example, *Easy–Difficult*. Different adjectives can be selected according to the teacher's interest. Originally devised by Osgood *et al.* (1957) it is often used as a personality trait or attitude measure outside the field of self-concept. Its main advantage is that it clarifies the adjective when the opposite is presented at the same time.

Q-SORT

Q-sort is a method that has been used extensively by Rogers (1970) in connection with client-centred counselling. It involves sorting into different piles a series of cards each containing a statement about the self; for example, 'I am always happy'.

The cards are ranked in order of how the person sees him/herself. A second ranking is made with the person considering how he/she would like to be. A prescribed set of 100 cards devised by Butler and Haigh (1954) is probably the one most frequently used.

Other variations of the method have included a list made up from the person's *own* past experiences and used mainly in clinical work. The literature to date lists around 22 different sets of cards which have been devised for various kinds of experiments. A big disadvantage in its use with children in the classroom is that it is very time consuming.

PROJECTIVE TECHNIQUE

Projective techniques have been used extensively in clinical work, the best known probably being the Rorschach inkblot test. The person is asked to say what picture he/she sees in the inkblot and the experimenter then interprets the response. Clearly, some training is necessary for the operation of this method. It has many critics in view of its subjective nature.

However, a more useful modern form of the method for use with children is the 'draw a person' test developed by Machover (1949). The child is simply asked to 'draw a person and then to include him/herself in the drawing'. The aim is to interpret the size and quality of the figures drawn in relation to the figure drawn to represent the child. Obviously, this is open to many criticisms of reliability and validity, but it is an interesting method with possibilities.

A variation of the projective technique is the 'sentence completions' test, when the person is asked to complete a partial sentence, for example, 'I feel shy when … '.

The main difficulty with all these projective techniques is the problem of devising a standardized scoring procedure. They reveal information of a more general nature than just self-esteem and do not easily lend themselves to use in the classroom.

OTHER QUESTIONNAIRES

Questionnaire methods are certainly the easiest to use with pupils in the classroom and are probably the most frequently used as a result. In addition to the Lawseq, there are several other questionnaires which have been well standardized. Unfortunately, most of them have been standardized on populations outside the United Kingdom. Amongst those worth considering are those of Coopersmith (1967) and Piers and Harris (1969).

THE PERSONAL INTERVIEW

Perhaps the most reliable method of assessing self-esteem is to find time to get to know a child personally, which of course is not always possible. If time could be made available for his purpose then a suitable informal interview is often the most reliable way to discover those areas in a child's life in which he/she feels insecure. The only real disadvantage to this method is that it is obviously not a standardized method and so cannot be used to give a measurement of self-esteem.

The interview should take the form of a friendly conversation, encouraging the child to talk more than the teacher. Although the interview should be informal, it is useful if the teacher has a ready-made list of areas to be covered, such as the child's hopes and fears, and attitudes towards significant people in the child's life. Further details of this method are given in Chapter 6 when discussing counselling techniques.

From this brief survey of some of the most popular methods of assessing self-esteem it can be appreciated that the whole area of assessment of self-esteem is still a contentious one. The problems are not only in the validity and reliability of the methods themselves but also in the inevitable limitations of the self-report method. However, for the teacher who may wish to pursue this topic further, perhaps from the point of view of a research project, the following references are recommended.

■ FURTHER READING■

Burns, R.B. (1979) *The Self-Concept: Theory, Measurement, Development, and Behaviour*, London, Longman.

Lawrence, D. (1982) Development of a self-esteem questionnaire, *British Journal of Education/Psychology*, Vol. 51, pp. 245–9.

Rosenberg, M., Schooler, C., Schoenbach, R. and Rosenberg, F. (1995) Global self-esteem, specific self-esteem: different concepts, different outcomes, *American Sociological Review*, Vol. 60, February, pp. 145–56.

Wells, L. and Marwell, G. (1982) *Self-esteem: Its Conceptualisation and Its Measurement*, London, Sage Publications.

Wylie, R. (1974) *The Self-concept*, 2nd edition, Lincoln, Nebraska, University of Nebraska Press.

Enhancing self-esteem whilst teaching

There has been ample research over the years illustrating the importance of the quality of the social interaction between teacher and child (Fontana, 1981). Overall, the evidence from this research is that where the interaction is positive the child achieves more and is better behaved. Judging from the results of this research into the quality of the teacher–child relationship, it would not seem unreasonable to assume that the teacher would be able also to influence self-esteem while teaching. The evidence is that teachers can influence the child's self-esteem while teaching (Lawrence, 1972a, 1973). It is not only that teaching is more effective when there is a positive relationship between teacher and child but also that the child's self-esteem is affected positively.

The work of Argyle (1994) drew attention to the factors involved in attitude change. Self-esteem is an attitude towards oneself. Argyle showed how attitudes are more easily influenced when the person who sets out to change attitudes has status and is capable of making a positive relationship with the subject. Teachers generally have status by virtue of their position in society, especially in the eyes of the children they teach. Those teachers who have status and also have a positive relationship with their pupils are likely to affect their self-esteem levels. The questions are what constitutes a positive child–teacher relationship and can it be taught? The remainder of this chapter sets out to answer these questions.

■ DESIRABLE PERSONAL QUALITIES ■

On the face of it, a positive relationship may seem to be merely a matter of being nice to children. However, it is more than this and it is to the work of Carl Rogers (1961) that we must turn to appreciate what is involved here. There are three personal characteristics considered by Rogers to be desirable qualities in a successful counsellor and it seems that the same qualities are involved in the establishment of a positive relationship in teaching. These qualities are described as 'acceptance', 'genuineness' and 'empathy'.

ACCEPTANCE

Acceptance means being non-judgemental of the child and accepting his/her personality as it is. But how can a teacher be non-judgemental when a child is misbehaving, one might ask? The answer is that the child is still accepted even though his/her behaviour needs criticism. Acceptance means the quality of being able to separate the 'deed' from the 'doer' so that the teacher focuses on the behaviour and not on the personality and character of the child. This is an important distinction and is outlined by Gordon (1970; 1974) who discusses the strategy of using 'I' messages and 'you' messages to maintain the distinction between the deed and the doer. This strategy is illustrated in the following two scenes.

Scene 1: reducing self-esteem

Teacher 'You are such a nuisance making a mess on the floor like this.'
Child 'I'm sorry.'
Teacher 'You are always doing it. You are always making this mess.'
Child 'I hate this school!'

In the above scene the teacher uses 'you' messages and so risks reducing the child's self-esteem as well as their future relationship. The main focus is on the child's character.

Scene 2: maintaining self-esteem

Teacher 'I am upset when I see this kind of mess on the floor.'
Child 'I'm sorry.'
Teacher 'This has happened before. I cannot walk over to the cupboard through this mess.'
Child 'Sorry, I'll clean it up.'

In this second scene the teacher uses 'I' messages and focuses on the situation, so maintaining self-esteem and the relationship. Even if the teacher's words are said with irritation, they are not personalized and, therefore, the relationship has not been threatened.

Children soon spot those who do not demonstrate acceptance. This is because children are particularly sensitive to non-verbal behaviour, or body language as it is sometimes called. Moreover, this non-verbal behaviour is normally outside one's conscious control so cannot easily be faked. The quality of acceptance has to be genuine and cannot easily be achieved through practice. It is more an attitude of mind and a personal philosophy. It means genuinely liking people, having a sincere respect for them and a firm belief in the potential ability of people to change. This quality usually develops gradually through life as people form their own philosophies. Its development is dependent mainly on the person having had an emotionally satisfying history themselves so that they have high self-esteem and naturally value and enjoy the company of other people. Although being accepting is not always easy for some people, it can be learned through intensive practice, providing that there is a sincere desire to change.

GENUINENESS

Genuineness is a quality that can be developed, although it demands an honest appraisal of one's own personality. This quality means being able to be spontaneous in social relationships without being defensive. It means being a 'real person' rather than hiding behind a 'professional mask'. To be this way a person has to have high self-esteem and so be able to reveal his/her personality without fear of rejection or disapproval. It means being assertive and able to express personal views and attitudes without fear. This is not easy when our greatest need is to be liked and when we know that we are not always as competent, skilful or likeable as we would like.

However, it is all too easy to succumb to the temptation of putting on an act. Carl Jung refers to this as 'wearing a persona'. People who do this regularly hide their 'human side' from others and the danger is that, if this becomes a habit, eventually, they hide it from themselves. This is undesirable on two counts: (1) it interferes with communication as people do not meet the real person and so do not really trust them; and (2) it is bad for mental health to be cut off from the real person in oneself. This can produce all manner of tensions. Examples of this can be found repeatedly in show business, where actors have to wear a persona in their chosen role.

We are faced with the cultural phenomenon of a high premium being placed on perfection in all things. To be genuine, therefore, will imply the ability to recognize that failure and success are relative terms and that in some sense we are all failures just as in some sense we are all successes. This quality can be learned with practice, as many successful assertiveness training workshops have proved. Genuineness is one of the characteristics of high self-esteem. This quality is discussed further in Chapter 12 along with suggestions to help teachers maintain and enhance their self-esteem.

EMPATHY

Empathy is a quality that means being able to appreciate what it feels like to be another person. Whilst none of us could ever know entirely what that would be like, we do have sufficient feelings and experiences in common to be able to 'get into another person's shoes' to some degree. Some people are more skilful at this than others, but with practice we can all refine this important skill of communication. Adults should be able more easily to empathize with children having at one time been children themselves!

The quality of empathy can be learned. One useful way of developing empathy is to begin to practise listening to the feelings behind a person's words. Usually we are so intent on understanding the verbal message that we can miss knowing just how the person is *feeling*. Our verbal reply can sometimes communicate that we have not really understood the emotional content of the message. The relationship would be all the weaker as a result.

Once a child feels that the teacher appreciates what it feels like to be them, they are 'on the teacher's wavelength'. As a result they are more likely to trust and to be influenced by the teacher. Rogers (1975) demonstrates a positive correlation between the degree of empathy displayed to a child and their level of school attainment. Putting this in simple terms, we all tend to do or perform better when we like the teacher and feel that the teacher likes us.

It is worth drawing attention at this juncture to the difference between empathy and identification, as the two can be easily confused. Whereas *empathy* means being able to appreciate what it feels like to be the other person, *identification* means actually behaving like the other person and feeling like the other person. In empathy, the teacher remains in the role of teacher and, so, in charge of the class, even though being able to understand the child's feelings. If there is identification with the child, the teacher becomes 'one of the kids', loses authority and becomes childlike. If the teacher is not sufficiently mature, with high self-esteem, there is always this danger when trying to appreciate the child's world.

Listening to feelings may prove to be difficult at times for the busy class teacher. Even simple listening to verbal messages can often be a problem without the extra effort demanded when listening to children's feelings. The distractions of a normal, healthy classroom are frequent and interruptions occur for many reasons. Consider how often an interruption occurs when the teacher is trying to converse with an individual child. A second child may suddenly demand attention for a host of possible reasons ranging from the reasonable to the deliberately disruptive. Visitors enter the room often unannounced. An event may occur outside the room which is momentarily distracting.

To be able to establish an empathic relationship with an individual child the teacher must try to guard against possible distractions. There is nothing more guaranteed to reduce self-esteem than when the person we are relating to suddenly turns his/her back on us.

AN EXAMPLE TO ILLUSTRATE THE QUALITY OF EMPATHY

In the following two scenes, two children are in distress. In the first scene, the teacher does not empathize with the child, and so the child remains with his distress unresolved. In the second scene, the teacher is aware of the importance of listening and reflecting feelings and, in doing so, the child's distress is relieved.

Scene 1

Teacher	Why are you crying, Peter?
Peter	It's nothing, Sir (*wiping his eyes*).
Teacher	There must be a reason. Tell me – I may be able to help [responding to the words only].
Peter	It's because I've just lost my pen my Dad bought me.
Teacher	Is that all? I can soon solve that problem. Here – have this one. It's new. I've had it for ages but I don't need it. [Dealing logically with the problem but ignoring feelings.]
Peter	Thank you, Sir (*begins to cry again*).
Teacher	Now what's the matter? [Unable to empathize.]
Peter	Nothing, Sir (*trying not to cry*).
Teacher	Now there must be something else wrong. You don't cry for nothing. What is it? Come now, tell me [continuing to respond logically and to ignore feelings].
Peter	I wish I hadn't lost my other pen (*more crying*).
Teacher	Now you are just being silly. I've given you mine which is just like the one you lost and you still cry [begins to be irritable as not able to empathize].
Peter	I want my pen that my Dad bought me (*sobbing*).
Teacher	Now that's enough. There's no need for that and I've listened to enough crying. Get on with your work [continues to be perplexed].
Peter	(*Trying to hide tears*) Yes, Sir.

Scene 2

Teacher	Why are you crying, Peter?

Peter   It's nothing, Sir (*wiping eyes*).

Teacher You seem unhappy [has listened to feelings].

Peter   I just lost my new pen my Dad bought me.

Teacher I understand. You must be feeling upset about that [communicates has understood].

Peter   (*Dries eyes*) It was terrible 'cos my Dad just bought it for my birthday and he hasn't a lot of money.

Teacher I expect you are feeling upset for him as well [continues to empathize].

Peter   Yes, he would be sad. A boy knocked it out of my hand and it fell into the lake.

Teacher I know your Dad, I bet he will understand how you feel [gives support through empathy].

Peter   Do you really, Sir?

Teacher He seems to be a very kind Dad, so I'm sure he'll be OK about it when you explain things. Accidents do happen [gives further support].

Peter   Yes, I suppose so (*brightening up*).

Teacher You're feeling much better about it now, aren't you? [Continues to empathize].

Peter   (*Smiling*) Yes, Sir.

Teacher By the way, you can have this one if you like – I've had it for ages, but I've never used it [responds logically to words now that he has empathized].

Peter   Thank you, Sir.

The teacher in the first scene was using an immediate and logical approach to the problem. The teacher in the second was using the quality of empathy to establish a relationship within which Peter would feel understood. The teacher in the first scene completely missed the real problem, which was, Peter's feelings for his father. A logical approach like that used by the second teacher was able to establish empathy by listening to the feelings behind the words. The solution was then not one of providing another pen, but rather of helping the boy to understand that he was not alone with his feelings.

■ TEACHER SELF-ESTEEM ■

The teacher with high self-esteem is likely to produce children with high self-esteem and also the converse. There is ample evidence to show that people who have positive attitudes towards themselves are also likely to have positive attitudes towards others (Omwake, 1954; Burns, 1975). The personal characteristics in the teacher, which contribute to the development of high self-esteem, have received some attention in the research (Maslow, 1954).

In addition to the qualities of empathy, acceptance and genuineness already mentioned, it seems that teachers who are able to delegate routine jobs, are able to find time to relate personally to the child, are tolerant of child's' conversations and are generally relaxed in their teaching are those who also have high self-esteem. This implies they are able to present a high self-esteem model with which the child can identify. It is interesting that this process of identification with the teacher is strongest where the child perceives the teacher as establishing a 'growth-producing atmosphere' (Murray, 1972). The topic of maintaining the self-esteem of the teacher is developed in more detail in Chapter 12.

■ COMMUNICATION ■

NON-VERBAL

As well as the teacher's personal characteristics affecting the child's self-esteem there are other factors within the control of the teacher which also can affect the self-esteem of the child. Amongst these the effect of the teacher's non-verbal behaviour is a particularly powerful influence. Children are very sensitive to non-verbal cues from others and apparently this sensitivity is reduced as the child develops so that the adult in comparison is often totally unaware of non-verbal cues.

Body posture, body orientation, eye contact, pauses in speech, tone and speed of speech, gestures, all can communicate different messages. Research has shown that these non-verbal cues communicate along three dimensions: the extent to which the person likes/dislikes; feels involved/non-involved; feels superior/inferior, to the other (Argyle, 1994).

Whereas verbal statements are generally more objective and can be manipulated, non-verbal behaviour cannot be so easily manipulated as it is more subjective and more instinctive. So, even if we try to hide our feelings of dislike, they will tend to be communicated non-verbally, especially to the person sensitive to non-verbal cues. If a teacher feels a child to be an unpleasant influence in the class but tries to make friends with the child by saying 'I like you', the chances are that the teacher's non-verbal behaviour will be saying the opposite.

The evidence is that when there is this conflict between the verbal and the non-verbal messages it is the non-verbal message that is heard. Teachers need, therefore, to check their sincerity – which means possessing the quality of acceptance as described previously.

VERBAL

It is more obvious that verbal messages can either enhance or reduce self-esteem. Staines (1958) identifies the words and phrases teachers use in the classroom, and finds that they could be classified into two groups: those that are encouraging, praising, valuing and generally relaxing; and those that are cajoling, blaming, punishing and generally anxiety-producing. The children's self-esteem and their levels of school attainment were higher in the first group.

It is fairly obvious that the words 'You have done well' are more likely to enhance self-esteem whilst 'You can do better than this' is less likely to do so. Of course, in each case the non-verbal behaviour which accompanies the words, is going to influence the final message. It is assumed that the statements in each case are made with sincerity. The conclusion from the Staines's research is that there is a positive and a negative way of saying the same thing and that which is used is crucial in determining its effects on self-esteem.

Teachers often ask whether all this means that the child should never be blamed or chastised. It should be stated categorically that enhancing self-esteem does not mean praising the child insincerely nor ignoring poor work or disruptive behaviour. With regard to poor attainments, no matter if the teacher does pretend that the child is doing well, the child very quickly compares him/herself with peers and obtains a realistic self-perception. This is why, even where some classes are grouped for ability, the children still know which are the 'clever' groups and which are the 'dull' ones even though there is an attempt to disguise this. For example, they may have tried to disguise the classification by calling the groups 'fishes' 'horses', 'rabbits', and so on, rather than classifying them A, B, C and D.

The main point here, however, is that teachers need to give a child a realistic self-concept, not a false one, and that when the relationship is a caring, trusting one, they will accept blame and criticism without this adversely affecting self-esteem (Sharp and Muller, 1978). Perhaps, more importantly, the teacher should be looking to praise effort and behaviour rather than attainment, although this raises the issue of how far a competitive atmosphere is potentially harmful. Clearly, when the child is being made overanxious by the need to compete then it is harmful for the development of his/her self-esteem.

The following two scenes illustrate the different ways in which a teacher can affect a child's self-esteem. The interaction in the first scene illustrates how the teacher reduced self-esteem while the second scene illustrates how the teacher maintained the child's self-esteem.

Scene 1: maintaining self-esteem

Teacher Come in, John. Sit down, please [communicates respect].

John Thank you, Sir.

Teacher Do you remember why I asked you to come to see me? [Gives opportunity to speak, so communicates trust.]

John Yes, Sir, because I've been in trouble again.

Teacher That's right. I thought we might have a chat about how best to help you settle down, as your behaviour is causing concern to a lot of people. What do you feel about it? [Separates the boy from the behaviour.]

John Yes, Sir. I suppose that's true sir.

Teacher I'm particularly worried in case your behaviour causes you to miss important parts of lessons and you might then have difficulties when it comes to exams. It would be a pity if you failed the exams, as you're an intelligent boy and could do well. Is there anything you'd like to tell me which you think I should know, as I think you look a bit nervous? [Emphasizes the positive; communicates trust.]

John   Yes, Sir. I can't do maths, Sir. I lost my maths book last term.

Teacher I see. Have you talked to the maths teacher about that? [Communicates trust.]

John   No, Sir. He doesn't know and I daren't tell him.

Teacher Would you like me to tell him for you? [Gives support.]

John   Would you, Sir?

Teacher Well of course, if you want me to [places responsibility for action on John].

John   Thank you, Sir.

Teacher If you have your book do you think your behaviour would improve? [Emphasizes the positive and potential for change.]

John   Yes, Sir, 'cos then I'd have something to do.

Teacher OK, John, let's see Mr Jones. I expect he'll be surprised to hear you've not been working because you lost the maths book [communicates understanding].

John   Yes, Sir.

Teacher Is there anything making you unhappy? We do want all the children here to be happy. Then they work well.

John   No, Sir, I like it here really.

Teacher OK, John. Thank you for coming to see me. Goodbye. [Closes with respect.]

John   Goodbye, Sir.

The teacher displayed:

- respect for John throughout the interview
- belief in John's ability to change
- positive attitudes
- good listening skills.

Scene 2: reducing self-esteem

Teacher Come in, Smith – sit down (*without looking up*) [no eye contact].

John Thank you, Sir (*sits on edge of chair*).

Teacher Now let me see. I told you to come and see me because you are a badly behaved boy. Do you understand? (*Voice rising*) [unable to separate boy from behaviour].

John Yes, Sir (*feeling frightened*).

Teacher You are the worst boy in the school, right? (*Voice harsh and aggressive.*)

John Yes, Sir.

Teacher I can't see you passing any exams or getting a good job when you leave with your sort of behaviour – what do you say? [No confidence in potential for change.]

John No, Sir.

Teacher So what are we going to do with you, eh? [No interest in John as a person.]

John I don't know, Sir.

Teacher Well, I'll tell you what. I'm giving you a chance to change before it's too late. I'm going to have you sit at the front of the class and I want you to come to my desk after every lesson. If you have been well behaved, I'll give you a star on this card. Understand? [Communicates lack of trust.]

John Yes, Sir.

Teacher Now if you have the sense to behave then you'll earn lots of these stars and when you have 20 of them I'll give you a reward. Do you understand me? [Communicates lack of trust.]

John Yes, Sir.

Teacher The reason I'm not expelling you from this school is because I think you just might be able to stop being stupid. If you don't stop, then out you go! See? [Emphasizes the negative.]

John Yes, Sir.

Teacher Now do you understand what I'm saying? [Communicates lack of trust.]

John Yes, Sir.

Teacher Right! Well, off you go. And for goodness sake try not to look so miserable. Anybody would think you were going to the gallows. Smile, for goodness sake [uses sarcasm].

John   Yes, Sir.

Teacher Get out! I've looked at you for long enough [confirms the negative] (*John scuttles out*).

The teacher displayed:

- lack of trust in potential to change
- lack of respect
- inability to empathize
- superiority of position through body language
- negative attitudes throughout
- use of sarcasm
- inability to separate John from behaviour
- no interest in John as a person
- no opportunity for John to contribute, because of poor listening skills.

■TEACHER'S PREFERRED TEACHING STYLE■

It is not only the teacher's attitude towards the child which affects self-esteem but the teacher's attitudes towards their particular teaching post and the organization of the school. In a famous study by Barker-Lunn (1970), it was found that teachers who believed in streaming for ability but had to teach in a mixed-ability situation generally had children with lower attainments and lower self-esteem. Moreover, teachers who believed in mixed-ability teaching and had to teach in a streamed situation also had similar results. It is interesting to reflect in this study that children of above-average ability were not so affected as those of average and below-average ability.

This question of the teacher being 'mismatched' is related to job satisfaction and in turn to stress and self-esteem.

■ EXPECTANCY EFFECTS ■

An aspect of the teacher–child relationship which has received a good deal of attention in the literature is that known as 'the expectancy effect'. This refers to the phenomenon that children tend to behave according to the teacher's belief in their worth. According to Hargreaves (1972) teachers generally have an 'ideal pupil' model, and those pupils in their care who do not conform to this ideal model are evaluated unfavourably and are not expected to perform well. The classical study of Rosenthal and Jacobson (1968) shows how this led to pupils fulfilling their teachers' expectations.

The work of Brophy and Good (1974) demonstrates how this occurs. It seems to be natural in all of us to want to classify and categorize people so that we know where we stand with them. Just as nature abhors a vacuum, so the psyche will fill in the missing information even if it is based on doubtful evidence. Brophy and Good show how teachers seek from the child's previous teacher, information with regard to work standard and behaviour and then operate on the assumption that the child will conform to this standard. They relate to the child as if they expect this behaviour. The present movement to avoid labelling children in the area of special education is also based on this kind of phenomenon.

Although it has been demonstrated in the research that the teacher may influence the child to behave in ways which the teacher expects, this will only occur where the relationship between them is a close one. Also, when the teacher's expectancies are radically different from the child's perceptions of his/her own behaviour, the evidence is that the teacher's expectations are ignored. So the expectancy effect does not occur in all circumstances. However, it is important that teachers are aware of the possibilities of it happening and so will be able to do something about it.

■ EVERYDAY CONTACTS ■

Although there are many aspects of the classroom environment which may influence the children's self-esteem, the research shows that it is the teacher's day-to-day contacts with the child which have the greatest effect.

In addition to the kinds of personal relationships already discussed, the teacher should try to ensure that some degree of personal contact is made with all children in the course of the day, even if this amounts only to a smile or one word of encouragement. This is easier, perhaps, for the primary teacher who has the children for most of the day, rather than for the secondary teacher who may have the child for only an hour a day or less.

It should be the aim of all teachers to get to know each child personally as soon as this is possible. However, this does not mean infringing their rights to privacy. Direct questioning about home life, for instance, should be avoided even when it may be suspected that all is not well there. In that case the teacher should give the child opportunity to communicate home details through the establishment of a caring, trusting relationship. Chapter 9 of this book contains a communication checklist to help teachers review their communication skills.

From the discussions presented in this chapter, it can be appreciated that all teachers are in a position to enhance self-esteem whilst teaching. Where teachers have high self-esteem and are genuine, empathic and accepting, and have status in the eyes of the child, they will automatically provide a self-esteem enhancing ethos in the classroom. For those children who have been identified as having low self-esteem and who may have other problems there are structured programmes that can be organized. These are outlined in the following two chapters.

■ FURTHER READING ■

Argyle, M. (1994) *Psychology of Interpersonal Behaviour*, Harmondsworth, Penguin Books.

Gordon, T. (1972) *Teacher-effectiveness Training*, New York, Wyden.

Hargie, R., Saunders, J. and Dickson, L. (1995) *Social Skills in Interpersonal Communication*, London, Routledge.

Neill, R. (1991) *Classroom Non-verbal Communication*, London, Routledge.

Priestly, P. and McGuire, J. (1986) *Learning to Help: Basic Skills Exercises*, London, Tavistock.

7

Small group activities to enhance self-esteem

The positive qualities of self-acceptance, respect for the needs of others and the ability to empathize are characteristics of the person with high self-esteem. Children in whom these characteristics are forming will be confident, enthusiastic for school and ready for new experiences. Most parents would probably agree that one of the ultimate aims of parenthood is to develop these qualities in their children.

Unfortunately, some children arrive at school without high self-esteem and are unprepared for the inevitable challenges they will face when first beginning school. Either they will be unsure of how to relate to the other children and remain on the fringes of a group or else they will be over-demanding of the teacher's time and jealous of other children. These are children who usually have low self-esteem. The chances are that these children not only have low self-esteem but almost certainly will have undeveloped ideal selves as well as probable undeveloped self-images.

Despite children beginning their school careers disadvantaged in this way, teachers can help them rediscover their self-esteem. Teachers are in a powerful position to influence children's self-esteem. The quality of the relationships that teachers establish with children will affect their self-esteem one way or the other.

Where there is an ethos of acceptance, and where teachers are able to be genuine and empathic, there will be a self-esteem enhancing ethos in their classrooms. However, for some children their self-esteem is so low that this approach will need to be supplemented with structured activities. It should be emphasized, however, that even where structured activities are used, those personal qualities in the teacher are still considered to be essential. No programmes or exercises will make the slightest difference to children's self-esteem if the teacher does not posses the qualities of acceptance, genuineness and empathy.

It is of some concern that there are some published programmes for self-esteem enhancement for use by teachers which appear to ignore this fact. It is doubtful whether programmes containing exercises and activities will make the slightest difference to a child's self-esteem without the teacher establishing a positive relationship with the children and providing them with a high self-esteem model. Within the context of this model there is research evidence that activities in the classroom do help children develop their self-esteem.

■ AIMS AND RATIONALE ■

The first aim of the activities is to allow children to express any feelings which they might normally feel unable to express either through a fear of punishment or through feelings of guilt. The low self-esteem child often lacks spontaneity. There is always the fear that expression of certain feelings, thoughts or ideas will result in disapproval or rejection. Through structured activities the child gradually learns that it is OK to have feelings and ideas, which are different from others, and that it does not mean the end of the world if he/she expresses them. Gradually, he/she learns the principle of individuality and learns to have confidence in being different.

The child with certain fears is able to receive the support of the group and may discover for the first time that he/she is not the only person with the same fear. It can be tremendously supportive to realize this.

The second aim is to give experiences of positive feedback. It can be a revelation to the low self-esteem child to hear somebody express positive thoughts about him/her: low self-esteem children are just not used to hearing these things. With these exercises they gradually begin to perceive themselves in a more positive light.

The third aim is to give opportunity for taking risks. The low self-esteem child cannot take risks either physically or in the sense of revealing his/her own personality. Such children often demonstrate a lack of confidence in all areas of their lives as low self-esteem so easily generalizes at this stage.

The fourth aim is to help children develop an acceptance of self no matter what limitations they may possess.

■ INTRODUCING THE ACTIVITIES ■

The way in which a self-esteem enhancement activity is introduced to the children can be crucial in determining its successful outcome. There have been cases where teachers have simply asked children to form a group and then began to work through the activities, with no preparation at all.

There are inevitably going to be anxieties surrounding the operation and these have to be dealt with. Without a proper introduction to the activity the children will be so suspicious of it that it will be almost impossible to establish their trust. Children, just like adults for that matter, can be suspicious of the motives of those who suddenly want them to discuss sensitive issues and to participate in emotionally toned activities. It is essential therefore that they are properly prepared for these activities.

The programmes outlined in this chapter are more suitable as a small group activity, and some children often feel more at ease in the small group. For these activities and for this type of child it is suggested that teachers explain to the pupils at the outset that the teacher has noticed that sometimes they do not appear to be very happy in class. As a result, it has been decided to try to help them feel better about themselves and about each other. The precise words used to communicate this message will depend on the age and intellect of the pupils concerned. In the experiments referred to in the Appendix, I simply said to the pupils (aged 8) that I was seeing them 'to ensure that they were happy in school'. A simple explanation is all that is required.

The activities outlined are suitable for all ages unless designated otherwise. Those that are suitable for a particular age only are designated either 'for primary' or 'for secondary'. Activities are for small groups unless designated 'whole school'.

ORGANIZING THE SESSIONS

1. Identify those children whose self-esteem has been assessed as below average. Include no more than eight children in the group.
2. Explain the programme to each child.
3. Do not insist that the children join the group where there is obvious resistance.
4. If a child resists taking part, try to engage him/her in an individual programme as described in Chapter 9.
5. Set rules for the group, for example, children must be polite at all times with no put-downs, children must raise their hands for permission to speak. Repeated breaking of the rules results in removal from the group.

Try to put together children of similar temperaments, that is, introverts and extroverts should not be mixed if possible. Try to include children of similar abilities. It would be unwise, for instance, to place a child with a learning difficulty alongside a high-flyer. Discussion is always smoother when the group comprises roughly pupils of the same intelligence level. This is not meant to imply that in other types of group, with different aims, mixed abilities should not work together. Indeed, there is a good case for arguing that pupils with particular handicaps should be integrated with non-handicapped pupils whenever possible. For the purpose of these activities, however, it is best to group like with like.

SEQUENCE OF ACTIVITIES

The following sequence of presentation of the exercises should be used. It is essential that they are administered in the order presented.

1. Trust activities.

2. Expression-of-feelings activities.

3. Positive feedback activities.

4. Risk-taking exercises.

THE ACTIVITIES

Self-esteem is often slow to change and teachers should be prepared for the programme to last a whole term. Each session should last no more than 45 minutes. The number of activities conducted under each of the four headings listed above will vary according to the needs of the group. Teachers will find that most groups need fewer sessions on the trust activities, perhaps requiring two sessions only, with equal time spent on the other activities spread over the remainder of the term. These are suggestions only, and drawn from the author's previous experiences.

■ TRUST ACTIVITIES■

Trusting means being secure enough to be able to express feelings and to be sufficiently secure with one another to be able to count on group support when taking risks. Clearly, the establishment of trust has to be a priority.

It is a good plan to begin the first session with a physical trust activity. Two examples of this type of activity are given below.

LEADING THE BLIND

Children work in pairs. One child is blindfolded while the other leads him/her around the school. Instructions are given that they must not lead their partner into danger. They each take turns at being blindfolded. After the session the group reassembles and a discussion takes place. The following questions should be asked:

■ What did it feel like to have to trust their partners while they were blindfolded?

■ Why is it that we are not able to trust some people but can easily trust others?

■ What qualities do we see in those we can trust?

■ What qualities do we see in those we cannot trust?

CATCHING THE BLINDFOLDED

The children are to work in pairs. Both are seated one behind the other. One child is blindfolded and sits waiting for instructions from the second child. The blindfolded child leans back with instruction for the second child to catch the first one, so preventing him/her from falling. The group reassembles and again the questions of trust are asked. This time the question should be put to the group whether the qualities present in those they trusted not to lead them into danger would be the same qualities they would expect to find in those to whom they feel they can confide.

■ RECOGNIZING AND DESCRIBING EMOTIONS ■

In order to be able to harness emotions and not let them control the child who experiences them, a child needs to be able to reflect on his/her emotions. This is not an easy process. First, it implies that the child has the necessary tools of intelligence, namely, the appropriate words. The following activity is designed to ensure that children have the correct vocabulary for describing their emotions.

ACTIVITY

Teacher has prepared a series of cards each of which has written on it a different emotion. For example:

Joy, sadness, curiosity, anger, guilt, fear.

Teacher asks for a volunteer to draw a single card from the pack without reading it. The teacher then reads out the card to the class and asks for two volunteers to act out the emotion written on the card without using speech.

The children are asked to write down in their notebooks the name of each emotion as it is recognized. The remainder of the cards are drawn until the pack is finished. When all the cards have been drawn and the children have finished writing down the recognized emotions a discussion can begin.

Amongst the topics discussed would be whether the expression of emotions needs speech for it to be recognizable. The children could be asked how they felt when witnessing these emotions. They might also ask how they might react if one of their friends were to show these emotions.

■ EXPRESSION OF EMOTIONS ■

A major block to high self-esteem is the repression of emotions. In Western society it is all too common to find people who are reluctant and some-times even afraid to express their feelings. It is a sad fact that some parents have felt a need to instil in their children the idea that certain feelings are unacceptable.

Whilst it is probably desirable that children are taught that some emo-tions are best expressed in private, it is a different matter to assert that chil-dren should not even accept that they have these feelings. How often do we hear a parent admonish their distressed child with the statement, 'There is no need to be upset! Don't cry. Only babies cry!'

This statement not only gives a message to the child that the parent disapproves of them, but it also conveys that there is something undesir-able over experiencing the emotion of distress. Consequently, the child may try hard not to cry and perhaps will pretend that they are not upset. Should this scene occur with any regularity, the child eventually would begin to deny the feeling of distress. But it is not humanly possible to extinguish emotions in this way. All that happens is that the emotion is repressed, in other words relegated to an unconscious feeling. The regular repression of emotions is well known to produce neurotic problems in later life. At the very least they can cause the person concerned to feel guilty about the sort of person they have become. Guilt is the enemy of high self-esteem. Accordingly particularly high value is placed upon the following activity designed to help children express emotions without guilt.

ACTIVITY

Children are asked to complete the following sentences in writing:

- I feel happy when …
- I feel sad when …
- I feel silly when …
- I feel angry when …
- I feel afraid when …
- I feel glad when …
- I feel proud when …

Teacher should ask children to put their names on their answer sheets and hand them in to the teacher. A class discussion could then be arranged with the aim of helping children accept their feelings without guilt. Children who have not been able to complete a sentence may either not have the necessary vocabulary or else they have an emotional block against expressing the emotion. Either way, the teacher should try to find time to discuss the results with the child concerned, in private after the session.

CIRCLE TIME

Children are asked to form a circle with the teacher included. The session is introduced as an opportunity for the children to say anything they like concerning school. They are encouraged to make positive comments as well as negative ones. It may be necessary for the teacher gently to draw out the more reticent members of the group. The teacher makes it clear that their comments will not be criticized or discussed with anybody else outside the session. Most children talk freely once they realize that the proceedings will remain confidential and that the teacher is non-critical. There are only two rules:

1. Nobody must laugh or scoff at anyone else's comments.
2. Permission to speak will be given by the teacher only on a raised hand.

RECALLING THE GOOD TIMES

Children are asked to recall a time when they felt especially happy. They are asked to close their eyes and visualize the scene. After a few minutes eyes are opened and volunteers are asked to tell the group what it felt like.

■ POSITIVE FEEDBACK ■

Children with low self-esteem rarely, if ever, hear anybody making positive comments about them. As a consequence they do not at first easily accept positive statements about themselves without some degree of embarrassment. Teachers should be prepared therefore for these exercises to result at first in defensive laughter and strong denial from the objects of any admiration. Despite this, eventually they will make a difference.

ANONYMOUS FEEDBACK

The children affix a sheet of paper on each other's backs and then approach one another informally to write on the owner's paper one positive comment about them. This continues until all have had a comment from every member of the group.

PUBLIC PRAISE

The children take it in turns to be the object of admiration from the rest of the group. Seated in a circle each member of the group makes one positive comment about the object of admiration. They are given 30 seconds to say something positive or else they are 'out'. The procedure can be continued a second and even a third time round with most of them having to drop out eventually and the remainder declared the winners.

POSITIVE POSTINGS

Each child has to write on one sheet of paper one statement saying why they like each other. The sheets of paper are then 'posted' to each other for them to take away and read at home.

■ TAKING RISKS ■

This is the final stage of small group activities and, provided the group has successfully completed the previous stages, improvements in confidence should be in evidence. The taking of risks is probably the most obvious distinction between the low self-esteem and the high self-esteem child. Consequently, these activities will provide the teacher with a measure of how much improvement in self-esteem has been made.

The ability to face life's many challenges is the mark of a high self-esteem person. This sometimes means being able to take calculated risks. The following activities introduce the children to risk-taking. This risk-taking involves both physical risk-taking as well as psychological risk-taking. The activities begin with physical risk-taking and end with psychological risk-taking.

PHYSICAL RISK ACTIVITIES

1. Children work in pairs. Each takes turns at carrying the other on their back across the room. Teacher should pair children so that there is no chance of a physical mismatch.
2. Each child is asked to climb a ladder or, ideally, up parallel bars in the school gymnasium.
3. Each child is asked to play the role of a goalkeeper while the other children in the group take turns at trying to score a goal from the penalty spot.

PLAYING THE EXPERT

Each child is prescribed a role to play in a short dramatic scene. The roles include explorer, map-reader, firefighter, cook, engineer and any others which the teacher may wish to include. Any suitable scene could be acted. The following scene has been found to be a popular one. Their task is to rescue an important person captured by outlaws and imprisoned in a remote castle. The castle is guarded by a ferocious animal and is situated on the opposite side of a river infested with crocodiles. The rules of this drama are as follows:

1. The experts have to be consulted before decisions are made in their area of expertise.

2. The expert's advice has to be taken without arguments by the others.

3. Nobody must mock any one.

PLAYING THE HERO/HEROINE

Children work in pairs and each takes turns at playing the role of a television news interviewer. The child is interviewed after having

1. been seen to rescue a drowning person in the sea;

2. just won an Olympic medal;

3. been seen scoring the winning goal in a school's football match; and

4. been the first child to travel to the moon and back.

ADDRESSING THE GROUP

Each child is asked to prepare a short five-minute talk to the group on any topic of his/her choosing. Teacher should give suggestions as to the topic. Most children will probably choose a hobby.

AFFIRMATIONS

At the end of each session it is useful for the group to close their eyes and say to themselves the following:

- 'I am a happy person.'
- 'I am a confident person.'
- 'I am not afraid.'
- 'People trust me.'
- 'I like me.'
- 'Other people like me.'

In the early stages, the teacher may have to say each sentence first with the children following in unison.

▇ FURTHER READING ▇

Canfield, J. and Wells, H. (1976) *One Hundred Ways to Enhance Self-concept in the Classroom*, Englewood Cliffs, NJ, Prentice-Hall.

Clark, J. (1978) *Self-Esteem: A Family Affair*, Minneapolis, MN, Winston.

Morris, E. and Morris, K. (1999) *The Powerhouse*, Bristol, Lucky Duck.

Rae, T. (1999) *Confidence, Assertiveness, Self-esteem*, Bristol, Lucky Duck.

Whole-school and whole-class approaches to enhancing self-esteem

The activities outlined in this chapter are suitable for the whole class so they can be incorporated into the school curriculum. Some children become unduly anxious when performing in the more intimate small group situation. The risk of this happening is minimized for those children when the activities are seen to be part of the normal school day.

The ultimate aim of the self-esteem enhancement activities suggested in this chapter is to develop in children the positive qualities of self-acceptance and respect for others so that the qualities become internalized. This means that they will not be dependent on external factors such as rewards from the teacher for their high self-esteem.

For most children, this internalization will be a very gradual process and teacher should not be dismayed if there are no quick changes. In the short term, particularly with primary age children, some of the listed activities may need to be supplemented at first with the use of external rewards in order to motivate change.

▓ WHOLE-SCHOOL APPROACHES▓

Research into the psychology of groups shows the importance of having a common aim as a significant factor in group morale (Argyle, 1994). When group morale is high, individuals' self-esteem also tends to be high. Any activities, therefore, which result in a building of morale in the school are likely to enhance self-esteem. The feeling of belonging to a worthwhile group should be the aim of the whole-school approach to self-esteem enhancement. The ways in which this can be achieved obviously will depend on many factors, including the type and size of the school as well as the neighbourhood. The following activities are amongst the means by which some schools have raised morale in this way.

SELF-ESTEEM THROUGH PHYSICAL PERFORMANCE

As most teachers know full well, the child who achieves in physical pursuits usually has high self-esteem. It is interesting to reflect on the high premium our society continues to place on physical prowess. How many children, or adults for that matter, would rather regularly represent their country in an international sport than achieve in some intellectual pursuit? Unfortunately, most of us lack the talent to be able to do this. However, we can go some way towards the same result through fun-runs, bike trials, school camps and so on.

Whatever activity is chosen the aim should be for the whole school to take part. Clearly this has to be organized so that the weaker members of the school do not suffer unduly. The fun-run could be organized so that each year-group completes a different part of the course, each part being of different lengths. Everybody who takes part should be presented with a certificate to that effect. If, in addition, a sponsor can be found, money could be earned or donated to a charity.

SELF-ESTEEM THROUGH THE SCHOOL CONCERT

The school concert or musical event is often a regular feature in a school's calendar but rarely does the whole school take part. This kind of event could be organized so that even those who do not actually perform on stage can still take a part in the production. If the event is made open to the public then it becomes easier to involve everybody, for example, classes taking turns at different performances to function as ushers. Once again, the essential aim is for the whole school to be involved and for there to be a tangible recognition of this. Each child could, for instance, be sent a letter of thanks afterwards.

■ CURRICULUM ACTIVITIES ■

Whereas all teaching can be organized within a self-esteem enhancement framework, some subjects can be intrinsically self-enhancing. Examples of these are music, art, drama and creative writing. If, in addition, children are given an opportunity to discuss their feelings when engaged in these activities, then further self-enhancement is possible.

■ DEVELOPING INTERNAL LOCUS OF CONTROL ■

The term 'locus of control' was first introduced by Rotter (1954). It refers to a dimension of personality which ranges from one extreme of a belief by an individual that whatever happens to him/her is not within his/her control. At the other extreme of the continuum, the individual believes that whatever happens to him/her is completely within his/her control. The former is known as being 'externally controlled' and the latter is known as being 'internally controlled'.

For an example of the internally controlled pupil, consider this likely comment on passing an examination: 'I expected to pass as I worked very hard and so I am not surprised at the results.' Failing the examination his/her comment might have been: 'I failed this examination because I am pretty stupid even though I worked hard.' It can be appreciated that the extreme position in both cases is perhaps unrealistic.

The externally controlled pupil might have said on passing the examination: 'I was very lucky, and anyway I think they were being kind to me.' The same pupil might have said on failing the examination: 'I failed because I had a rotten teacher.' Clearly some degree of internality is preferable to externality.

For the purpose of self-esteem enhancement it is useful to know that there is a positive correlation between internality, self-esteem and achievement. We should aim therefore to help pupils achieve some feeling of control over their destinies. In the classroom this can be developed in three main ways:

1. Through pupils having some say in their own governance, that is, the setting up of class rules.
2. Through giving opportunities for pupils to record and evaluate their own progress.
3. By giving pupils some opportunities to initiate their own learning.

In a joint study (Lawrence and Blagg, 1974) a group of children who were allowed to control part of their remedial reading sessions through reading games showed greater gains in both reading and self-esteem than other matched groups. Although locus of control was not measured in that particular study, a number of studies have shown how teachers can teach pupils to become more 'internal' and, in turn, increase their attainments (de Charms, 1976).

In class discussions, teachers should encourage pupils to be critical of their own learning environment and the ways in which their learning is organized. The aim should be to help them become responsible for their own behaviour, with regard, of course, to their stage of development. It would be unrealistic, for instance, to expect the first-year primary child to be able to discuss the organization of the classroom without having had the experience of working in groups.

■ ACTIVE TUTORIAL WORK ■

In Chapter 1 we referred to the symbolic interactionist view of the 'self' concept. People in general are group dependent, and self-concept is formed partly by social interaction. As the classroom comprises a particular group, the teacher is in an ideal position to be able to structure the group to the best advantage of the pupils.

The primary aim of the classroom group normally is academic achievement but, as all teachers know, social learning takes place at the same time as the pupils interact with one another. In active tutorial work, the learning of social interaction is the main focus. This kind of group activity is similar to circle time but differs in two important respects. First, it is more structured in that the teacher has a clear teaching objective, for example, to help pupils appreciate the dangers of smoking. Secondly, the teacher takes a more prominent role and acts as a model.

CONDUCTING THE SESSION

Following a brief introduction by the teacher on the aims of the session, the class is asked to comment. Various views will be expressed, some of them in a disparaging way. The teacher must be alert for that kind of comment which can be self-esteem reducing for some members of the class.

The teacher should deal with a 'put down' by modelling the appropriate behaviour. In this way the teacher takes a more dominant role than in circle time. Negative views should be discussed objectively. Sooner or later the teacher will be asked for his/her views, and the teacher should be open and spontaneous, and able to express opinions easily without prejudice or defensive behaviour.

Sometimes silences will occur. They can be used positively as when thinking of a particular point which has just been raised. When they become uncomfortable they should be discussed openly. It is of note that, in general, children are more easily able to tolerate silences than are adults.

When conflicts occur or when members become hostile, it is important for the teacher to intervene to keep the discussion on the topic but without discouraging the expression of feelings. A conflict is an ideal opportunity for the teacher to model the desired behaviour. Pupils can learn much from the mature, high self-esteem teacher who handles this kind of situation effectively, for example, by demonstrating that it is OK to have opposing views, indeed people are perfectly entitled to do so, but there is no need for them to become personal. The activity below (p. 107) on resolving conflicts might be introduced if a conflict does occur.

The key to these activities is the maturity of the teacher. It may seem to some teachers to be a threatening experience but it is well worth the risks. When successful it becomes a growth-producing experience both for the pupils and the teacher.

■ DEVELOPING CRITICAL THINKING SKILLS ■

One characteristic of the high self-esteem person is the ability to become self-determinate. The high self-esteem, self-determinate person, would make up his/her own mind when having to make a decision. For instance, they would not necessarily accept the advice of another person without first having critically analysed the situation themselves. In order to do this analysis they would have to be able to be logical in their thinking.

The powerful influence of advertising is an example of how important it is that children learn to be analytical and logical in their thinking. The following activity uses the medium of some common advertisements that have appeared in the media to give practice in analysing the claims of popular advertising. This activity is probably more suitable for the upper primary or post-primary school student.

ACTIVITY

Teacher displays the following advertisements on a board or overhead projector:

> Eat an apple a day. It will help you grow strong bones.
> Buy my ice-cream! It is the creamiest in the world.
> This exercise machine will help you grow 10 cms in height in 2 weeks.
> Eating fish-oil will prevent arthritis in later life.

Notes: Other advertisements of the teacher's choice could be substituted.

The class should ideally work in small groups to discuss each advertisement. Each group should have an elected leader. The teacher gives the children instructions to discuss whether they believe the advertisement and whether they have enough evidence to make a decision. If they need more evidence they should discus how they would set about finding the evidence. After 10 minutes' discussion there is a plenary session in which each group leader reports back to the class the results of their discussion. The teacher guides the discussion at this stage.

■DEVELOPING A SELF-IMAGE■

This activity is probably only suitable for the early primary school child. Self-image development in children begins first as a gradual awareness of their physical characteristics. Awareness of mental characteristics comes second and may not develop at all in some children!

ACTIVITY

Working in pairs, each child should be given a large clean sheet of paper on which to lie down. The children take turns in lying down while the second child draws around their body. Alternatively, hands and feet may be outlined, and even painted, to demonstrate size, variety, similarity and individuality. The teacher should try to visit each pair to make positive comments on the drawings.

On completion of this activity the children are asked to compare themselves with each other. Teacher may need to reassure some children over their efforts, for example, 'good things often come in small parcels'.

■RESPECT FOR INDIVIDUAL DIFFERENCES■

It could be argued that respect for people who are different from ourselves is a characteristic of a civilized society. This means respect not only for differences of race or religion, but also for physical and personality differences in people. Respect for others is a characteristic of the high self-esteem person.

The following activities are designed to encourage children to respect individual differences. A first step in respecting differences in other people is to understand them. The first activity is therefore aimed at helping children *understand* why people can be different from themselves.

ACTIVITY

Ideally, a member of the class from a different ethnic group to the rest should be asked to give a short talk on their origins. If there is no member of the class from a minority ethnic group perhaps an outsider could be invited to do the talk. After the short talk the following questions could be put to the speaker.

- How do other people treat you?
- Are you aware that you are different?
- What makes you happy?
- What makes you sad?
- What could other people do to make you feel happy?
- Do you feel you belong here?
- How would you help other newcomers from your country settle?
- What is the main difference between you and us?
- In what ways are we alike?

■ BULLYING ■

The child who bullies is so often the child who has been bullied, either at home or at school. In the following activities children role-play experience of both being bullied and doing the bullying. The aim of the activity is to help children develop the quality of empathy.

ACTIVITY

Children work in small groups with one member of the group acting as the bully whilst another member of the group acts as the victim. It is suggested that the bullying take the form of verbal abuse. The remainder of the group observe.

Following the role-play the group discusses the scene. They are asked to comment on the following questions:

- How would they would feel if they were bullied this way?
- How do they think the bully must feel?
- Why is it that some children are bullies?
- What should a child do if bullied?

Schools generally have a policy on bullying. The teacher offers suggestions on how to cope with bullying based on their school's bullying policy. The session might be concluded by asking any children who might be concerned about being bullied to speak to the teacher later.

■ COOPERATIVE BEHAVIOUR ■

Children are naturally competitive. It seems that the need to compete is innate in all organisms. Observation of animals reveals that they all have a 'pecking order'. Pigeons, for instance, seem to know instinctively who should be first at the food. It is the quality of cooperation that has to be learned.

Children with high self-esteem find it easier to cooperate. They have no need to continue to assert themselves or to strive to be first in any pursuit. This is not meant to imply that their naturally assertive behaviour is inhibited. It means that in the high self-esteem child the drive to compete is under control and is only asserted in appropriate circumstances, for example, in an organized game. Children can be helped to appreciate the value of cooperation. The following activity gives practice in cooperation.

ACTIVITY

The class is split into small groups and a leader is appointed for each group. Each group is assigned a corner of either the sports field or playground so that they are not likely to intrude on one another's performance. The leaders have been previously briefed to devise a plan with their group to cross a deep river thought to be crocodile infested.

The group leader has to organize the building of a boat, making oars, organizing refreshments, keeping watch for the crocodiles, steering the boat, manning the oars, and so on.

The activity should take no more than 20 minutes after which time there is a class discussion on the activity. Teacher directs the discussion to focus on how far they cooperated, why some did not cooperate and what they would do next time to ensure maximum cooperation.

■ ASSERTIVE BEHAVIOUR ■

The high self-esteem child is an assertive child but not an aggressive one. Assertion is the opposite of being submissive. It means being able to express feelings and thoughts appropriately and without fear. Being assertive means being able to state clearly what you want without fear and being able to repeat it exactly even if your request is refused. This is different from being aggressive and rudely demanding attention. The following list illustrates the difference between the three attitudes:

Aggressive	Assertive	Submissive
Rude	Polite	Humble
Unpleasant	Pleasant	Servile
Arrogant	Confident	Timid

ACTIVITY

The class observes whilst selected children role-play, working in groups of three. Each child in the group takes a turn at practising being assertive, being the teacher and being the observer.

The task of the observer is to note behaviour under three headings – feelings, actions and behaviour. The scene is the sports field where a teacher has decided that one of the children is to be dropped from the football team as not being properly fit. The group is given two different scenes to role-play.

Scene 1. The child reacts to the news with dismay and becomes angry.

Immediately after the first scene the teacher introduces a class discussion focusing on the words used in the scene. It is explained to the class that the words 'I', 'When' and 'Because' should be used.

The rationale behind this choice of words should also be explained. The words are the same as those outlined in Chapter 6 from the Gordon model. Suggestions are made for an assertive response using the Gordon model.

Scene 2. The child reacts with assertive behaviour.

The following scenes may be used in the role-play.

Scene 1

Teacher	'I have decided that it is best for you, John, not to play today as I believe you are not fully fit after your recent illness.'
John	'That's not fair! I'm OK! I can play.'
Teacher	'Sorry, John, I have made up my mind.'
John	(*getting angry*) 'You are not fair. I could play with no problem.'
Teacher	'It's no use being upset John. You are not playing'
John	'You are not being fair. You don't want me 'cos you want to play another person.'
Teacher	(*walking away*) 'I'll see you later John.'
John	(*very angry*) 'I'm not going to play in this team ever again, so there.'
Teacher	(*now also angry*) 'If that's how you feel you may as well go inside now.'

Scene 2

Teacher	'I have decided that it is best for you, John, not to play today as I believe you are not really fully fit after your recent illness.'
John	'I feel fit enough.'
Teacher	'Sorry John but I don't think that you are fit.'

John   'I could prove I am fit if you would allow it.'
Teacher   'I still don't think you are fit.'
John   'I would appreciate a chance to show you how fit I am by running, if you don't mind.'
Teacher   'OK. Let's see if you can run around the oval.'
John   'Thank you.'
Teacher   'OK, you may play in the team.'

These two scenes could be analysed as follows:

Scene 1
    Feelings: Anger.
    Thinking: The teacher thinks I am no good.
    Behaviour: Walks away in defeat.

Scene 2
    Feelings: Concern
    Thinking: The teacher does not know how fit I am.
    Behaviour: Proves the point by running.

ACTIVITY

Children work in small groups and are asked to write down the words they might use in the following scenes to demonstrate assertive behaviour.

1. Another child has borrowed your pen and not returned it as arranged.
2. Your parents want you to run an errand to the shops but you are watching your favourite television programme.
3. Your teacher asks you to stay behind after school to finish some work but your parents have arranged to pick you up after school to take you to see a football match.
4. You have bought a comic at the local newsagents but on opening it at home you find that two pages are missing.

Teacher organizes a whole class discussion on their results after the activity and recapitulates on the activities summarizing the technique.

■ CONFLICT RESOLUTION ■

The scenes outlined above under the assertive behaviour activity are also examples of possible conflicts. The activity below gives further practice in assertive behaviour but this time the focus is on the conflict itself.

ACTIVITY

Children are asked to role-play the following scene in pairs in front of the class.

The first child has discovered that the second child is using a pen that the first child lost a few weeks ago and feels that it should be returned to its rightful owner.

The children rehearse the following guidelines and plan their dialogue before acting out the scene.

PREPARATION: Rehearse the words, focusing on the problem situation or the problem behaviour, that is, do not attack the other person. It is the situation that is the problem and not the child.

CLARIFICATION: You state your concern using 'I' messages and then invite the other child to do the same.

REFLECTIVE LISTENING: You communicate empathy by listening to their feelings about the matter, that is, you let the other child know that you know how they are feeling.

NEGOTIATION: Both parties re-state what they see as the problem but without personal criticism.

SOLUTION NEGOTIATION: Ask the other child for their solution if it is different from yours.

■ TEACHING RELAXATION ■

There is research evidence to demonstrate the value of teaching relaxation techniques to children. Immediately following a relaxation procedure it is discovered that children are better behaved and are able to concentrate for longer periods on their work. There are many different kinds of relaxation procedures.

The following procedure is one devised by the author, which has been used successfully with both children and adults. Children are asked to:

Sit comfortably and remove your shoes.

Raise your eyes (not the head) to the ceiling.

Focus on a point on the ceiling until your eyes become tired.

Close your eyes.

Think of your toes and wriggle them.

Think of your ankle joints and relax them.

Think of your calf muscles and relax them.

Think of your knee joints and relax them.

Think of your thigh muscles and relax them.

Think of your side muscles and relax them.

Think of your shoulder muscles and relax them.

Relax your neck muscles.

Relax your facial muscles.

Let your jaw drop and relax the tongue.

Relax your chest muscles.

Relax your stomach muscles.

Think of your breathing (remind children that it happens automatically).

Let 'it' breathe in and out as it wants to and when it wants to.

After every breath out say the word 'relax' quietly to yourself.

Now imagine a scene where you are always happy and 'see' yourself in it.

■ SETTING GOALS ■

High self-esteem children are able to extend themselves in their thinking so that they are able to make plans for the future. The following activity gives practice in this.

ACTIVITY

Each child is asked to make two lists. The first list contains plans for the immediate future, for example, activities for the next few days. The second list contains plans for when they leave school.

Volunteers are asked to read out their lists. Nobody is forced to do this. The class is previously briefed not to mock anybody and to respect everybody's right to have their own list of activities.

REMINDER

Whatever activities or exercises are used these should be organized and implemented within the framework of acceptance and respect for the student, which was discussed in Chapter 6. It is a case of 'not what you do, but the way that you do it'. That quotation is even more apt when considering setting up an individual programme as described in the next chapter.

■ FURTHER READING■

Barbra, M. and Barbra, A. (1978) *Self-esteem: A Classroom Affair*, Minneapolis, MN, Winston.

Everhart, R.B. (1985) On feeling good about oneself: practical ideology in schools of choice, *Sociological Education*, Vol. 58, pp. 251–60.

Flowers, J.V. (1991) A behavioural method of increasing self-confidence in elementary school children: treatment and modelling results, *British Journal of Educational Psychology*, Vol. 61, pp. 13–18.

Robinson, G. and Maines, B. (1997) *Crying For Help: The No Blame Approach to Bullying*, Bristol, Lucky Duck.

Woolfe, R. and Dryden, W. (eds) (1996) *Handbook of Counselling Psychology*, London, Sage.

Individual programme for enhancing self-esteem

A structured individual progammme for a child's self-esteem enhancement is presented in this chapter. Some children with low self-esteem are not suited to participating in group activities. They may either be anxious about doing so, finding the group situation stressful, or they may be too disruptive for group activities. Whatever the reason, some children would benefit from an individual approach to self-esteem enhancement.

The rationale for the programme is based on the author's research into self-esteem enhancement that uses a self-concept theory approach. The programme consists of weekly, individual sessions, with selected children, over a period of 10 weeks. As the programme does not demand the insights or training of the professional counsellor the sessions could be carried out by suitably selected non-professionals. This approach requires those conducting the programme to be suitable briefed on self-concept theory and given suggested guidelines on how to conduct the sessions.

At the initial briefing, it is explained that the programme is aimed at changing the negative self-attitudes of the children involved. It is not aimed in the strict counselling sense of helping children resolve any possible emotional or behavioural difficulties. Should there be some children who do demonstrate problems of this nature the professional supervising the programme should be informed, and appropriate action would be taken. The school psychologist might need to be involved in the child's further treatment.

▓ RATIONALE ▓

The individual programme for enhancing self-esteem outlined in this chapter is in many ways a replication of an ideal parent–child relationship. It is an attempt to combine the theories of Rogers (1951) and Bandura (1977), who have described how parental and child relationships can be enhanced. Although the programme does not necessarily demand professional training, it acknowledges the need for particular personal communication skills. Provided the appropriate warm, caring and empathetic relationship is established, the child will model on the person conducting the programme. There is some evidence from an experiment with adults, that when a person makes a conscious effort to think about another person with whom they have a caring and warm relationship, they are better able to cope with life's adversities (Sedikides and Kumashiro, 2005). The authors of this research are unclear why this should occur but the individual self-esteem enhancement programme, as outlined in this chapter, is probably a further illustration of this phenomenon. This accords with the work of the social psychologist Argyle (1987) who showed how close relationships with another person contributed to their total well-being. Many people would observe this phenomenon in their everyday lives and agree with these researchers. The children in the author's research, where similar relationships were established, were no exception to this. These children who received regular treatment from a caring adult, where a warm relationship was established, showed rises in self-esteem. This is the main principle on which the individual self-esteem enhancement programme is based.

▓ WHO SHOULD CONDUCT THE PROGRAMME? ▓

In the author's experiments, non-professionals conducted the programme. This study was not meant to imply that the individual self-esteem enhancement programme should be conducted only by non-professionals. Teachers who possess the qualities of acceptance, genuineness and empathy, to a greater or lesser degree, should be even more skilled than the non-professional at this kind of work. It is the qualities of the person conducting the programme that are the keys to enhancing self-esteem and not necessarily their professional training (Carkhuff and Truax, 1967).

■ USING NON-PROFESSIONALS ■

If the decision is made to use non-professional people for the individual self-esteem enhancement programme, it is important to select these people carefully. Although it is possible to select through the various personality questionnaires available (Rogers, 1961), it is suggested that, apart from the unreliability factors inherent in most methods, to have a formal selection procedure has dangers and could prove to be counterproductive. It would be potentially harmful to reject those who do not achieve the required score on the personality tests.

The selection of non-professionals would, therefore, be made informally on the basis that they are already known to the school as sympathetic to the needs of children without being sentimental. Additionally, they should be without any signs of obvious emotional ill health and, where possible, be emotionally spontaneous. To be able to select people on these criteria requires an intimate knowledge of them. In the author's experiments, the selection was left to the heads of the schools. Those selected for the programme were sometimes parents of the children in the school, but always people known and recommended by the head of the school.

When it has been decided to use non-professionals, it is essential that they are prepared to consider the principles outlined in this book and are briefed on at least four separate occasions before the programme begins. Perhaps the local school psychologist would be available to do this and also to meet the non-professionals from time to time to monitor the programme.

Whilst this is not essential, when the teacher has time to do it, in practice it is always best if the teacher is able to call on the services of another professional for support. Whatever is decided upon in this context, it is absolutely imperative that the non-professionals be properly vetted according to official regulations of the school. For example, they may have to receive police clearance before being allowed to work with children.

Ideally, it should be the school counsellor who conducts the programme but not all schools have the luxury of having a trained counsellor on their staff. This kind of work could be done by a teaching assistant. As referred to above, a suitably briefed non-professional person with appropriate personal qualities might easily do this kind of work.

For the purpose of discussion, it is assumed in this chapter that it is the teacher who is conducting the programme.

■ SELECTING THE CHILD ■

The kind of child who responds best to this individual programme is generally the one who is able to reflect on their behaviour and then take action on the reflection. In selecting the child with low self-esteem, it is theoretically possible to select by standardized methods. However, as discussed in Chapter 5, perhaps the best way to get to know if a child has low self-esteem is to know that child personally. The difficulties of assessing self-esteem were also addressed in Chapter 5. Even so, it is wise to employ some kind of measure of progress to discuss the results with the child's parents as well as for one's own professional satisfaction.

In some instances a child may decline the offer of this programme. There are probably many reasons why this might happen but the usual one would be because the child felt some degree of embarrassment. If this happens it may even be advisable to suggest that he/she bring along a friend. Interviewing children in pairs has also been shown in experiments to be successful although, if this is the determined format, the programme may need some modification. Clearly, the relationships may not necessarily be so intense.

It is always advisable before offering the programme to consider whether the particular child in question might be more suited to the class activities outlined in the previous chapter. The more extroverted children are the ones most suited to the class activities and probably less suited to this individual approach. The final decision should be made on personal knowledge of the child as well as on his/her self-esteem level.

■SEEKING PARENTAL PERMISSION■

Before deciding to offer the programme to an individual child, it is imperative that the child's parents are approached for their permission to conduct the programme and also to discuss with them the reasons why their child has been selected for the programme. It should be explained that the aim would be to help the child change negative self-attitudes and develop high self-esteem so that the child becomes happier in school.

■THE STATUS OF PROGRAMME PROVIDER AND THE SETTING■

The work of researchers, such as Argyle (1994), shows that in addition to needing to be able to establish a warm, caring relationship, those who more easily are able to change attitudes also have *status*. This means that the child should feel that the programme provider is important. For example, the child will feel important by virtue of having an 'important friend'. Translated into practice this implies that the programme should take place in a comfortable, well-furnished room and that the person conducting the programme should be introduced properly by the head of the school.

The issue of status raises once again the point mentioned in Chapter 6 in connection with the teacher's self-esteem, that is, the importance of genuineness. The teacher should be genuine and spontaneous. In this way he/she will bring into the conversations his/her own lifestyle and interests. This again serves the purpose of making the child feel important.

■INTRODUCING THE SESSIONS TO THE CHILD■

The manner in which the sessions are to be introduced to the child is important and care should be taken to do this before the first session. Whatever is said to the child should be said in a non-threatening, low-key manner. The details of the introduction will depend on the age and maturity of the child but in general the following words are suggested:

'I am trying to see as many children as I can to ensure that they are happy in school and, as it is not easy to talk in front of others in the class, I am seeing children by themselves where possible. Would you like to come along every week?' This is a fairly innocuous introduction, but it does convey that the teacher is interested in the child's welfare and is not intending to test or to teach.

The teacher should also remember the non-verbal cues which the child will be aware of; for example, the introduction should be accompanied with a smile. A child's response is usually positive where the teacher has the necessary personal qualities conducive to effective communication, as outlined in Chapter 6.

It should be stated, however, that there are aspects of the teacher's previous relationship with the child which may interfere with conducting this kind of work. The child is likely to have perceived the teacher as an authority figure and it may take a few sessions before the child is able to accept the different non-judgemental relationship. The teacher should be prepared, therefore, for this response and not become anxious about it. Sometimes this may be a serious impediment to the programme, in which case it is advisable to enlist a teacher from another class to do it or even to introduce a non-professional, as in the experiments referred to earlier. Whether the teacher or a non-professional is used, there are certain principles which should be observed.

■ PRINCIPLES OF THE PROGRAMME ■

For many children this programme is probably a strange experience as they have the luxury of one adult to value and listen to them. As a result they may be a little suspicious at first and be uncommunicative. It is essential that the teacher is prepared for this kind of reaction and does not immediately begin forcing the child to talk.

It should be communicated to the child that the teacher knows that it is sometimes difficult to know what to say. Instead of pursuing the topic a game might be introduced or a drink and a biscuit suggested. Anything that will reduce tension should be used. The essential point is to divert the interview into a more relaxed channel. Eventually the child will realize the unique nature of the interview and that it is not threatening. The teacher should, of course, explain that it is confidential.

One aim of the programme should be to help the child express feelings. However, it can be damaging to self-esteem to force people to 'get it off your chest'. This is a commonly heard exhortation, but unless the individual is ready and trusts the person he/she is communicating with, it can be inferior-inducing. We all need a private world and if another enters it without invitation we feel threatened.

One aim of the programme should be to provide a trusting relationship within which the child can feel free to confide his/her innermost feelings *should he/she wish to do so*. Statements such as 'Tell me about your parents!' should be avoided even if the teacher has reason to believe that things are not right at home. Instead, the teacher might say, 'Sometimes children find it hard to settle in school because they are thinking about their family'. This gives the child the opportunity to say something about his/her family if he/she wants to. It also allows the child to change the topic if he/she wishes.

PERSONALITY CLASHES

One reason for misunderstandings between people lies in their different temperaments. We have all had the experience of not being able to relate easily to somebody without really knowing why this is so. We may say 'I can't get on his wavelength', and this is sometimes referred to as a 'personality clash'. The teacher should be prepared for this to occur from time to time.

Common amongst the differences in personality is that between the introvert and the extrovert. Consider how often we have heard an introvert saying about an extrovert, 'Don't trust *that* one. Hail-fellow-well-met. No depth'. The extrovert will also be likely to say, 'Don't trust *that* one. Still waters run deep'. Each mistrusts the other because they cannot understand the other's perspective on life. When this clash occurs between teacher and child it is wise to accept it and perhaps use another person to do the activity.

AVOID PATRONIZING

There is always the danger of sounding patronizing when caring about somebody in distress. The teacher should beware showing the child *sympathy* when what is needed is *understanding*. Sympathy can so easily degenerate into a sentimental sharing of emotions with nothing being done to enhance self-esteem. The aim of this programme is to influence the child's attitudes towards a positive self-appraisal. Admittedly, the child will bask in the warm emotions which sympathy portrays, but this is merely indulgence and in no way contributes to a more positive self-appraisal.

When a child does show negative feelings towards self, for example, 'I'm no good', the teacher should obviously support the child over the circumstances but should not do so in a maudlin or pitying way. That kind of comment should be met preferably with a reflection of the mood that was behind the statement to show empathy and then a discussion on the reasons for the statement. If it is seen subsequently as a manifestation of a general feeling of unworthiness and with no rational basis, the teacher should change to a more positive topic.

SHOWING INTEREST

The low self-esteem child is unused to having the luxury of finding an important adult who is prepared to listen to them and who also finds them interesting. It is all too easy to miss the significance of the child's need to feel that he/she has a worthwhile opinion. Be on the alert therefore for the smallest signs of an opinion from the child and comment on it by actually saying, 'That is an interesting thing to say'.

Beware also the many distractions which can occur when trying to concentrate on the child's comments. There is nothing more inferior-inducing than being told to 'Wait a minute while I deal with this'. The child should expect to have the teacher's full attention during the programme session.

We have all had the experience, surely, of colleagues or companions being distracted when we are trying to obtain their attention. Sometimes they are distracted by their own thoughts, as when remembering an appointment and then looking at their watch instead of looking at us! Whilst for most people this would be just dismissed as an irritation, for people of low self-esteem it serves to confirm to them that they are inferior.

LENGTH OF SESSIONS

Most children require around five minutes to adjust to the session. After a further 30 minutes or so they tend to become restless. It is suggested from experience that each session lasts 40 minutes. It is important to inform the child of this at the outset of the programme and to adhere to it.

One main reason for a set time is to avoid the situation where the teacher will have to decide arbitrarily that time is up and so leave the child sometimes wondering if it was something that occurred during the interview which had caused the teacher to end it just at that point. Accordingly, it is wise to warn the child that there are 10 minutes left so he/she is not unprepared for the completion of the session.

Once the first session has been completed it will be helpful if the teacher completes the communications checklist outlined below, to review their own behaviour during the session with the child. The insights gained from this procedure should make it easier to structure the remaining sessions.

Communications checklist

Non-verbal behaviour

Do you tend to adopt a 'closed manner' when addressing the child, for example, arms folded?

Do you use eye contact?

Do you smile a lot?

Is your voice harsh and aggressive?

Listening skills

Do you allow yourself to be distracted?

Are you able to guess the child's feelings when he/she talks to you?

Do you 'feed back' to the child the feelings you guess?

Are you able to paraphrase the child's words as an aid to empathy?

(continued)

Establishing trust

Are you able to show the child that you trust him/her?

Are you able to express your own feelings freely?

Does the child know the kind of person you are?

Do you communicate that you are interested in the child as a person?

Being positive

Are you able to manage difficult behaviour without reducing self-esteem?

Are you able to change your negative thoughts to positive ones?

Do you find yourself using more negative than positive phrases?

Do you have a wide variety of positive phrases and words or only a few?

Developing expectancies

Do you communicate that you have confidence in the child's ability to learn?

Do you communicate that you expect the child to behave appropriately?

Are you able to communicate expectancies without 'commands' and without 'preaching'?

Are you able to encourage independent thinking in the child?

CONTENTS OF A SESSION

The contents of the sessions will depend on the personality and interests of the children as well as their maturity level. Some children will chat freely, whereas others will need the stimulus of another medium such as a book or a game. Whatever medium is used, it is the *quality* of the relationship which will determine its successful outcome and not the *content*.

The aim is to seek every opportunity to value the child and this is best done through the teacher showing pleasure in the child's company. Where the child may present negative or even unpleasant comments it should be remembered that beneath the unpleasant exterior there is probably a low self-esteem, inadequate child. This means the teacher will be able to tolerate and accept the child even though not approving of the behaviour.

The conversation should then take the form of discussing the negative comments within an atmosphere of trust and acceptance. When possible the teacher should attempt to give the child insight into his/her behaviour but without adopting a judgemental attitude. Suggestions should be offered, for instance, rather than advice given.

■ TERMINATING THE PROGRAMME ■

It is difficult to be precise regarding the number of sessions the child will need. Ideally, they should continue as long as the child obviously needs them. This is usually shorter than the length of the time the child is continuing to enjoy them. Whilst a permanent programme would probably be enjoyable for most children, it is interesting to observe how they look forward to the sessions. The teacher must seek the opinions of colleagues as well as being guided by his/her own observations as to the number of sessions.

Once a decision has been made to discontinue the programme it is essential that the child is informed of this decision in such a way that it is not perceived by the child as rejection. Reference should be made to the child's apparent improvement obviating the need for further interviews. Moreover, it is always best to begin to discontinue the programme gradually, for example, weekly sessions becoming fortnightly sessions, and then going to once a month until eventually they cease altogether.

At the final session the child should be informed that he/she and the teacher will always remain friends and that the child should remember to come to see the teacher at a personal level when needed. The teacher need not fear that this is going to result in further impromptu sessions; experience has shown that this happens only when the child genuinely does have a further problem.

If the decision to terminate the sessions has been made wisely, then the child will no longer need to come and further contact can remain at the same level of personal involvement as with the rest of the class during everyday teaching.

■ A TEN-WEEK PROGRAMME ■

The following is a suggested format for the individual programme within which there is room for invention. The programme should be flexible and not to be regarded as a rigid schedule of weekly events, as the essence of the programme is its spontaneity. Deviations from this suggested format are bound to occur as the child progresses and converstion begins to flow more freely.

To recapitulate, it is impossible to be wholly prescriptive with this kind of self-esteem enhancement programme. The above programme is a suggested framework only. Spontaneity, flexibility and enthusiasm are the essence of the programme. In some instances it may need to be used as it stands, particularly during the first few sessions and where a child may be either reticent or reluctant to communicate. The precise format and content of each session could also vary according to the individual child's level of intelligence and specific areas of concern. The overall aim should be to encourage children to express themselves verbally and to confide in the teacher so that they able to express their hopes and fears without criticism. The games should be regarded as media for this verbal expression. Most children communicate verbally more easily while having fun.

Week 1

The child is introduced to the programme and made to feel welcome and helped to relax. It is explained that they will meet once a week for a while during which they will play games and have a chat. The teacher should have a pack of cards and maybe a paper and pencil at hand, and suggest that they play a game.

Week 2

The child could be asked to tell the teacher of anything good they did during the week. Ask if anybody had commented on good things about them. Conclude with a game again.

Week 3

The teacher should by now have formed an idea of some positive qualities in the child and should comment on them. This should be genuine. Conclude with a game or by asking the child for a drawing.

Week 4

The child is asked to tell the teacher of anything bad that happened to him/her during the week and also of anything good. This should be discussed positively. Conclude with the usual game or drawing.

Week 5

The teacher asks the child what they would like to do when they grow up. Suggestions could be made. Teacher should ask the child to decide whether a game or a drawing should be done.

Week 6

The teacher should discuss with the child how to relax . A suitable relaxation exercise should be explained and practised. Again, the session ends with a game or a drawing.

Week 7

The teacher and child discuss why some people are not good at making friends. The session concludes with drawing up a list of qualities that people find in those who are friends.

Week 8

The teacher and the child discuss things that make people scared. They conclude by listing the qualities in people they admire.

Week 9

The teacher introduces the topic of bullying in schools; why some people are bullied and why some people do the bullying. The session ends with positive solutions to the bullying problem.

Week 10

The teacher introduces the topic of self-esteem by defining it and asking the child how he/she rates. The teacher suggests ways in which the child might begin to feel happier about him/herself.

Throughout these sessions the child will be modeling their behaviour on the teacher who should be empathetic, enthusiastic, relaxed and fun-loving. This assumes that the teacher has high self-esteem. Chapter 12 discusses how teachers might be helped to maintain their level of self-esteem and to reduce the inevitable stresses involved in teaching.

■ PEER SUPPORT AND BEFRIENDING PROGRAMMES ■

In addition, or instead of, an individual self-esteem enhancement programme a school might prefer to consider a peer support programme. If this decision is made the children chosen to participate in the sessions should also be briefed in the same way that the non-professional helpers were briefed.

Children have always supported and consoled each other, automatically and informally, over various problems. However, this has been put on a formal basis in some schools where formal befriending programmes are in operation. A particular child is detailed to support and befriend another child. The child in need may, for instance, be a newcomer to the school or have specific emotional or behavioral problems that require help. The child who does the befriending usually has been appropriately briefed. Children used in this role are usually empowered to the extent that they also benefit from experience in this supportive role. There is evidence that their self-esteem rises and they become more accepting and less judgemental of others.

■ FURTHER READING ■

Cowie, H. and Pecherek, A. (1994) *Counselling Approaches and Issues in Education*, London, Fulton.

Harris, T. (1969) *I'm OK – You're OK*, London, Pan Books.

Priestley, P. and McGuire, J. (1986) *Learning To Help*, London, Tavistock Publications.

Robinson, G. and Maines, B. (1997) *Crying for Help: The No Blame Approach to Bullying*, Bristol, Lucky Duck.

Rogers, C. (1951) *Client-centered Therapy*, Boston, MA, Houghton Mifflin.

10

Challenging behaviour

Surveys into the sources of stress in teaching regularly quote having to cope with challenging behaviour in the classroom as a major concern. Whilst those teachers who have high self-esteem are more likely to be able to cope than teachers with low self-esteem, children with severe emotional and behavioural problems often require intensive treatment. In the not too distant past, treatment usually meant referral to a child guidance clinic and the child would be seen outside the school. More recently some doubt has been cast on the effectiveness of that traditional approach and evidence has accumulated to indicate that more often than not the best person to do the 'treatment' is the class teacher, and the best setting for the treatment is in the situation where the problems occur, that is, the classroom. Some challenging behaviour arises simply as a result of poor class-control strategies and not because of a problem within the child. Unfortunately, it is all too easy to regard the problems as arising within the child and for sanctions that reduce self-esteem to be applied to the child.

A full account of treatment for helping those children with major behavioural difficulties lies outside the scope of this book. However, the framework within which helping strategies should be applied to many children's difficulties is certainly associated with the topic of self-esteem.

Teacher's relationships with children communicate acceptance or rejection even though he/she may not always be aware of this. When a child impinges on the teacher in an unpleasant way there is always the danger of dealing with the behaviour in such a way that reduces self-esteem. When this happens the problem can so easily escalate.

Before considering methods of dealing with challenging behaviour, it is important to emphasize that enhancing self-esteem is not inconsistent with good discipline. A concern for some teachers has been that by focusing on the quality of their relationship they are in some danger of losing their authority. This is a fallacy, although an understandable concern. It is only where the teacher *identifies* rather than *empathizes* with the child that problems with discipline can occur.

Teachers must remain in charge of their classroom! The teacher has to learn to communicate to the child that his/her problems are understood and that the teacher knows what it feels like to be that child (empathy), but not to the extent that the teacher loses his/her identity as the person in charge.

There are many methods of achieving class control. Whatever methods are used the aim should be that ultimately the child should take responsibility for his/her own behaviour. This will occur sooner or later, depending on the age and maturity of the child, provided that the teacher is able to maintain control without reducing self-esteem.

The following scenarios are presented as examples of some of the most common types of challenging behaviour encountered by teachers in the classroom. Suggestions are made on general strategies to use whilst maintaining the teacher's and the child's self-esteem.

■ THE DISRUPTIVE CHILD ■

When a child is disruptive in the classroom, the manner and words used by the teacher will affect the child's self-esteem. When it is possible to control the child's behaviour without reducing self-esteem the future relationship between teacher and child will not be placed at risk.

The method suggested here is similar to that recommended by Gordon (1974). The main focus in the Gordon method is on the particular words used. This focus is on the words 'I' 'when' and 'because'. The rationale behind these words is as follows:

'I' 'WHEN' AND 'BECAUSE'

'I' – allows the teacher to express his/her own feeling. It also lets the child know how his/her behaviour is affecting the teacher. Some children are unaware that their behaviour has an adverse affect on their teacher.

'When' – focuses on the situation and not on the child. It also allows the child an escape route implying that their behavour is only criticized in that situation.

'Because' – brings rational argument into an emotional situation. It demonstrates to the child that their behaviour is not being challenged simply at the whim of the teacher but that it has a logical reason.

AN EXAMPLE OF REDUCING SELF-ESTEEM

A child has accidentally upset the contents of your bookcase. Books and equipment are strewn all over the floor and you are naturally upset. The child hurriedly picks them up and replaces them in any order.

Teacher	You are stupid. Why didn't you look where you were going? [Uses 'you' message.]
Child	Sorry.
Teacher	You really are an idiot! You never think before doing anything.
Child	Sorry.
Teacher	You really are clumsy, but never mind. You'll grow up one day, I expect.
Child	(*Mumbling quietly*) Huh! I hate this place. [Child responds negatively feeling under attack.]

It is clear that in this scene the child feels under attack as a person. This is because of the teacher's frequent use of the word 'you'. Moreover, the child has no way of being able to demonstrate regret or to learn appropriate behaviour if the situation were to occur again. There is no room for rational discussion.

EXAMPLE OF MAINTAINING SELF-ESTEEM

Teacher   I feel so angry when that kind of thing happens as I can never find books easily when they are out of order like that.

Child   Sorry.

Teacher   When I need a book quickly and I find it's not where I expect to find it, I get really cross [uses I-when-because].

Child   Sorry, I'll put them back properly for you. [Child responds positively as not under attack.]

Teacher   Oh! I'll help you. It'll be quicker if we both do it together.

Child   I really am sorry. I didn't do it on purpose.

Teacher   I know. Don't worry – it's just that I get annoyed when I can't find anything.

Child   I'll try not to put them out of order.

Teacher   Thanks. We'll soon put them back.

Child   (*Mumbling quietly*) I must try not to do it again.

In this second example self-esteem is maintained. The reason for this is that the child did not feel under threat as a person. The focus of the teacher's anger was on the child's behaviour. This encounter illustrates the principles of the Gordon method using the words 'I', 'when' and 'because'.

THE CHILD WHO IS MISCHIEVOUS BUT HAPPY

Children often 'test out the teacher' to see how far they can go before the teacher sets the limits. This is seen more often in the primary school child but also in the immature secondary age child. Children have no natural sense of knowing how to behave appropriately. This kind of child is gleefully mischievous and can cause considerable disruption. As a result, the teacher is likely to feel considerable irritation in return.

It is suggested here that in the interests of establishing a genuine relationship as well as in the interests of the teacher's self-esteem, this irritation should be expressed and not hidden. It is the way in which it is expressed that is important. Once again, the irritation needs to be expressed in such a way that conveys that it is the behaviour of the child that is the object of the teacher's concern and not the child. This is a subtle but important difference.

This is once again an illustration of the Gordon method of using 'I', 'when' and 'because'. The teacher might in this situation say, 'I am angry when I see paper thrown around the room. I cannot organize the room with so much rubbish on the floor'. Usually at this point the child will respond with appropriate behaviour. If instead of these words the following were used, 'You are being silly', then the child immediately recognizes the personal attack and self-esteem is threatened. The whole situation then is in danger of escalation.

Using this approach for the mischievous child will usually be sufficient to establish order. This is not meant to imply that the child's misbehaviour will not be repeated. Some children may need further reminders about the consequences of their behaviour before conforming. They may need a more systematic approach. In the example discussed here it is the 'surface behaviour' which is the topic of control. But it will at least allow the lesson to continue.

Where further, more extensive, treatment is indicated, management of the behaviour should involve combining a counselling approach with the principles of behaviour modification. The counselling principles are outlined in Chapter 9. In addition, the teacher should devise a reward system for child. Every opportunity should then be taken to praise and reward him/her for acceptable behaviour. The child should be asked to keep his/her own record of this behaviour. The aim of doing this would be to help the child become internally controlled. The reason for this approach is that there is a positive correlation between locus of control (see Chapter 8) and self-esteem. The record of positive behaviour might take the form of a chart on which the teacher would agree to record the child's desirable behaviour at the end of each lesson.

Summary of treatment features

- Maintain self-esteem by using the Gordon model.
- Use the counselling principles outlined in Chapter 9.

■ Devise a behaviour modification chart to record positive behavour.

■ A chart should be kept by the child to change locus of control.

■ The chart should be presented to the teacher at the end of each lesson.

THE CHILD WHO APPEARS TENSE AND UNHAPPY

There is a second kind of disruptive behaviour. This is the child who is not enjoying being disruptive and who appears tense and perhaps is depressed. The immediate aim for the teacher is to 'take the heat out' of the situation. This child is probably in a highly emotional state and already of low self-esteem.

Bearing in mind again the need not to reduce self-esteem, the teacher needs to reassure the child that he/she knows how the child is feeling. This means empathizing with the child. The teacher might say 'I understand that you are unhappy' or 'I can see that you are feeling miserable about this'. The child is likely to recognize an attempt to see things from his/her point of view and generally will calm down a degree. After that, the teacher should offer to discuss with the child the reasons for the problem, but at the end of the lesson. Again, this allows the lesson to continue and is dealing at this juncture with the 'surface behaviour only'.

If the teacher had applied appropriate sanctions this would have only served to reduce self-esteem. Whilst there is a place in class control for punishment, having to rely on punishment as the only method of control means, usually, that the teacher is unable to establish the caring atmosphere recommended. Class control based on self-esteem enhancement will use positive methods, with the teacher providing a calm, high self-esteem model. There will be a healthy learning environment within which the children will feel free to ask questions and to take risks as they learn new skills. They will not be afraid of failing as they use trial-and-error learning, and will gain in confidence as they are allowed to work at their own pace and receive the teacher's approval for effort.

In contrast, a teacher who relies only on punishments to control the class may indeed have a quiet, well-behaved class but the children's natural curiosity will remain inhibited. When they are confronted outside with disruptive behaviour in others they will likely respond in terms of the model they have learned in the classroom. They have been taught aggression.

Consistent with this self-esteem enhancement approach to behavioural difficulties is the belief that children are potentially capable of controlling their own behaviour. This is in contrast to the view that implies that children with disturbing behaviour cannot help themselves. It should be stated here that children who come under that category are rarer than used to be thought and form approximately only 1 per cent of all cases referred to educational psychologists.

It can usually be assumed therefore that the child can be held responsible for his/her behaviour even if it may need the teacher to organize a regular counselling programme to enable the child to gain insight. When that is indicated it should always be done in conjunction with the school psychologist or social worker. Once a child is able to establish a caring relationship with a teacher very often the child's problems clear up. Research points to the significance of this kind of relationship in a school when a childs' home background may be disturbed (Rutter *et al.*, 1979). The incidence of challenging behaviour has a stronger association with the quality of the teacher–child relationships in a school than with the child's socio-economic background. It is not justifiable to comment that a child's adjustment is dependent upon the home situation when confronted with a behavioural difficulty. Whatever the background, the evidence is very clearly in favour of the view that 'schools do make a difference'.

▧ DEFENCE MECHANISMS AGAINST LOW SELF-ESTEEM ▧

Prevention' is better than 'cure' and the occurrence of many challenging behaviours could be minimized through the establishment of the kind of positive and caring learning environment which is the main theme of this book. There are some children, however, who will present challenging behaviours no matter how much effort is put in by the teacher to prevent them. Since the days of Sigmund Freud, it has been recognized that sometimes we behave in an irrational manner as a result of unconscious conflicts. Some children may receive threats to their self-esteem emanating from outside the classroom but which are unconsciously expressed as behaviour difficulties within the classroom.

Most of us at some time or other have been victims of the 'kick the cat' syndrome. We may have had a bad day and arrive home tired and frustrated. We feel bad-tempered; unfortunately our aggression is taken out on the nearest object. Of course, we feel guilty immediately afterwards, knowing we have behaved irrationally.

Children can be subject to the same phenomenon. There are many different kinds of defence reactions, all attempting in some way to compensate for threats to self-esteem. The following are some of them.

BELITTLING AND BLAMING OTHERS

Most teachers have encountered the pupil who continually blames others for his/her difficulties. Jane was in her third year of secondary school and, although performing at an average level in most subjects, she was not a popular girl. Her behaviour towards the teacher was usually polite but she was always complaining to the teacher that other girls were preventing her from working, or that they were not working properly themselves.

Not surprisingly, people quickly lost patience with her and the teacher began to apply sanctions whenever she was out of her seat to complain. This made matters worse and the climax came when she threw her books across the room in a fury having been told by the teacher that she would have to remain behind after school to complete unfinished work.

Wisely, the teacher avoided a confrontation seeing that the girl was out of control; the teacher picked it up with the comment 'We can talk about this after school', and quickly changed the topic, addressing the whole class. This had the desired effect of calming the girl, and not losing face in front of the class.

This example serves to illustrate how some pupils' behaviour quickly escalates from being at first only mildly irritating. Mildly irritating behaviour like this should be investigated early when it is seen to be persisting, as it can often be, as in this case, a sign of some deeper unconscious conflict.

The example also serves to illustrate that low self-esteem is often manifested by a need to blame others for one's own feelings of inadequacy.

Treatment

Following this scene Jane was interviewed after school by the teacher. The teacher has attended a course on counselling and was well aware of the need to establish a trusting relationship and to maintain Jane's self-esteem. At first she was resistant to discussing anything but gradually relaxed as she became aware that this was not a punitive interview. She agreed to talk further with the teacher the next day and a series of sessions were arranged.

It transpired that at home Jane had always felt inferior to her sister who was younger but seemed to be brighter. Basically, she had a good relationship with her sister so never felt able to express negative feelings. Also, her parents made her feel guilty if ever she showed signs of aggression towards her sister. Aggression was therefore repressed but came out in school when with other girls, who probably unconsciously reminded Jane of her relationship with her sister.

With Jane's consent her parents were seen by the teacher and they were helped to see how she was developing low self-esteem. They agreed to discuss the problem with a social worker who aimed to help them modify their attitudes towards Jane.

The teacher continued to counsel Jane to help her take responsibility for her own behaviour as well as helping her regain lost self-respect. She began to interfere with other girls' work a lot less frequently and as a result began to gain their respect. As the weeks passed Jane improved out of all recognition as she was able to see that she had been her own worst enemy in the past, and as her parents began to give her more value.

LYING AND BOASTFUL BEHAVIOUR

John was in his last year at primary school. He was performing at a slightly below-average level in schoolwork but was quite popular with the class. His only real problem was that he regularly told the most outrageous stories and tended to boast about his exploits. The other pupils just laughed at John's stories but new teachers were always taken in at first, for example, 'I went hang-gliding at the weekend with my Dad. We went on the same glider and swooped over the city houses'.

During class discussion periods John always tried to dominate with further tall stories. Sooner or later the class would become scornful and the teacher sarcastic. He would then burst into tears still protesting he was telling the truth. The situation became worse as time went on, until he began to live most of the time it seemed in a fantasy world.

His parents were seen by the teacher and confessed to having the same problems with him at home. It was a happy family and there was no obvious reason for the boy's difficult behaviour. But it was clear that John was forever trying to say, in effect, 'Take notice of me! I am important!'

John's case serves as an example of how low self-esteem can be masked by an apparent confidence. Despite the boy's accounts of his exploits it was obvious to all that beneath his brash exterior he felt very inadequate.

Treatment

It is not always possible to establish the causes of challenging behaviour, as in John's case. But it is not always necessary to have to do so if we consider the case from a self-concept theory viewpoint. Here we have a boy who needed a quick boost to his self-esteem and who had to be helped to appreciate the impact on others of his lying.

As with Jane's case, the treatment centred on, first, the establishment of a trusting relationship between John and his teacher within which he felt able to confide. As he came to trust the teacher he was able to accept the teacher's view that his behaviour had been undesirable and to take responsibility in changing it.

Changes did not occur immediately and whenever he told tall tales thereafter teacher and parent would treat it lightly and quickly change the subject, as distinct from their previous reactions which had been punitive. He was learning a more 'realistic self-image'.

DAYDREAMING

Peter was 9 years old and working well below average in schoolwork. He had been referred for a psychological examination with the possibility of a transfer to a special school for slow-learning children. Testing, however, revealed an ability far above that which he had been showing.

Discussion with the class teacher revealed that he daydreamed a lot and was exasperating in that he invariably produced a blank sheet of paper at the end of the lesson when all the other children had done at least four or five sides of work. Peter had been chastised regularly and became used to being punished for 'lack of effort and laziness'.

This is a classical example of the low self-esteem child lacking confidence and so performing as though of low ability. Peter had opted for avoidance of what he felt to be a potentially humiliating experience. To describe any child as lazy is an evasion of a diagnosis and this was no exception. He scored at a very low level on the Lawseq self-esteem questionnaire and clearly had very little confidence in himself.

It is better to risk the teacher's punishments than to be humiliated in public by being seen to fail. This kind of case often 'represses' the feelings of inadequacy, or in everyday language 'he has shut off'.

Treatment

The school psychologist organized counselling and self-esteem enhancement activities as a starter. Soon Peter began taking more notice of his surroundings and to begin to attempt to work. At that point remedial reading was arranged as he was now in a more positive frame of mind to benefit from it. The teacher changed her attitude towards Peter once the diagnosis had been communicated to her, and began to encourage and praise him for the slightest sign of effort.

His parents had accepted that in their opinion he would never achieve very much but after meeting the school social worker, they began to see these signs of progress. They were encouraged by the social worker to adopt a more positive and encouraging attitude. Special school was no longer considered to be a viable option and the child engaged happily in his present school.

■ SEEKING THE POSITIVE FEATURES IN THE CHILD ■

What should be done about the child whose behaviour and achievements are not obviously capable of being praised? Does the teacher risk reducing self-esteem by ignoring the child or risk and possibly also communicating dislike through non-verbal behaviour? The answer to these questions have been given already with regard to the desirable quality of acceptance which is conducive to self-esteem enhancement. To recapitulate, acceptance means being able to accept the child even if not the behaviour. The teacher might like to practise the following acceptance activity in order to begin to establish some positive rapport for the child.

SUGGESTED ACCEPTANCE ACTIVITY FOR THE TEACHER

The activity is to complete a list of five positive statements about behaviour that can be applied to the child. The next step will be to gradually communicate these statements to the child in conversation.

The following list of statements are examples only as the precise words will vary with the child and the situation:

'I like your cheerful smile'.

'I can see that you have put a lot of effort into doing this work.'

'I have noticed how popular you are with other children.'

'Thank you for helping me with that task today.'

'I like the way you always keep your desk and yourself neat and tidy.'

The teacher will need sometimes to reflect deeply on his/her own behaviour before being able to do this. Where it is difficult to accept the child, the question must be asked: 'What is it in me that prevents me from giving this child respect even though I do not approve of the behaviour?'

OVERT AGGRESSION AND BULLYING

Thomas was in Year 2 of secondary school. His academic record had always been poor although he had always excelled on the sport's field. He was a natural footballer, being strong, fast and well coordinated. He made no secret of the fact that he was aiming one day to become a professional footballer. One might have expected him to have been popular with other boys in view of this sporting talent. Unfortunately, he bullied others and most children were afraid of him. In class he was often sullen and rude to teachers and was often on report.

Events came to a head on the day he physically attacked a teacher. The teacher in question had arrived at the classroom to find uproar and Thomas banging the head of a smaller boy against the wall. The teacher tried to intervene only to receive a violent blow on the arm himself. Fortunately, the teacher wisely recognized that Thomas had lost control of himself so left the room for aid. He returned a few minutes later accompanied by the deputy head of the school only to find the class quiet and Thomas apparently reading a book.

Subsequently a psychological interview was arranged with the school psychologist. It was revealed that Thomas was virtually illiterate with a reading age of only 6 years and of very low self-esteem. The parents were also seen by the school social worker and a history taken. Thomas had suffered prolonged absence from primary school owing to illnesses and had fallen behind in the basic school subjects.

Remedial reading had been arranged from time to time but he had never really benefited from this. The parents were cooperative but were dismayed and surprised to learn of his reading retardation. Apparently he had always been inclined to be moody at home whenever school was imminent.

This case illustrates that for some children remedial reading is not sufficient in itself. Thomas was a typical case where a change in attitude needed to occur before he was able to benefit from the reading instruction. His low self-esteem prevented him from believing he was capable of learning, and no positive reinforcement could help him on that first rung of the ladder of success.

The case also illustrates how low self-esteem results from failure in a specific area which is regarded as important by the significant people in the child's life. In Thomas's case it was the area of reading. It also illustrates how success in a particular area does not necessarily compensate for low self-esteem in other areas. Academic success is the main focus of most schools and self-esteem comes mainly from that area.

In Thomas's school success on the football field was not valued very highly even though he excelled at it. If he had not bullied others it is possible that he might have been able to compensate to some degree by receiving positive feedback from the school with regard to his football ability.

As things stood he received no positive feedback in any direction. Even his parents did not value his football as they were not interested in sport.

Treatment

Once again a caring, totally accepting relationship needed to be established before Thomas could be helped. The teacher was far too busy and committed in other directions to take on this task but fortunately the school psychologist and social worker were able to effect the change. Eventually Thomas was able to take responsibility for his behaviour and to make an effort to change it.

At the same time a further attempt was made to provide remedial reading. This time it was organized within a self-concept theory framework, that is, self-initiation and self-checking games were used with the aid of a computer so that Thomas did not have to worry about being seen to fail in front of others. His motivation was much greater this time and soon he began to make progress. Reading materials concerned with football were provided when possible.

The following year his football ability came to the notice of the local football association outside school and his self-esteem began to rise as his talent became more widely known and more genuinely admired by his parents, teachers and, eventually, by his peers.

THE SCHOOL REFUSER

Sometimes a pupil has frequent absences from school for no known reason. In desperation the parents seek a medical opinion and are dismayed to be told that the cause is psychological. The child becomes anxious when having to face attendance at school. These cases have traditionally been known as 'school phobics', although this is probably a misnomer as most schools these days are pleasant places in which to work. The term *school refuser* is therefore to be preferred.

Derek was 6 years of age and had been attending school for only one year, but during that time had achieved only 40 per cent attendance. Usually his mother had supplied a medical certificate stating that her son was suffering from either migraine or stomach ache. Eventually the GP suggested a visit to the psychologist. He had noticed that Derek's problems appeared only when school was imminent.

The psychological examination revealed a very close-knit family, with Derek the only child. Although born prematurely and for a time a sickly child, he was now healthy and had no health problems apart from these regular headaches and stomach aches at school times.

The mother was described as overanxious. She continued to worry about Derek's health despite reassurance that he was a healthy boy. Whenever Derek felt he had a headache the mother confessed to worrying in case he had a serious illness and she herself ended up with a headache. The father was concerned but took a rather passive role in the family preferring to leave decisions to his wife. He idolized Derek, who could do no wrong in his eyes. There was little doubt that both parents had met Derek's every need from birth and he had had no demands made on him at all.

The irregular school attendance had begun when Derek complained to his mother that another child in his class had hit him and given him a headache. Without enquiring further his mother had suggested he stay away from school that day until he felt better. Derek jumped at the suggestion and so the pattern of absences begin. He had learned that to avoid school he had to have a headache. When he was persuaded to return he developed genuine aches and pains through anxiety.

It is a well-established phenomenon that by avoiding a fearful situation it can be blown up in the imagination out of all proportion to the original event. When forced to attend school he found it stressful to have to share the teacher's attention with 25 other children. It was clear that this boy had received feedback at home which told him he was 'the most important person in the world', as a result of which he had developed a most unrealistic self-image.

This case illustrates the point made in Chapter 4 that we all feel secure behaving in ways which fit in with our image of ourselves. In this case Derek was not able to behave at school as if he was the most important person in the world. Consequently he felt anxious and insecure. Some degree of dissonance is inevitable as the two situations are different and most children quickly accommodate and integrate the new experiences of school into their developing self-images. In cases such as Derek's the contrast between home and school was far too radical for easy assimilation.

Treatment

The main focus on treatment was helping Derek achieve a realistic self-image. To enable this to happen meant enlisting the cooperation of the teacher and the parents. The teacher was asked to give Derek a little extra attention whilst the parents, in comparison with their previous treatment of the boy, were asked to make more demands on him. The mother required lengthy counselling to help her do this and also to help her prepare to use firmness in getting Derek to school as, even though cooperation had been promised, Derek was still going to have to face up to that first attendance.

As predicted he threw a temper outburst; his parents remained calm but firm and Derek calmed down as soon as he was bundled into the classroom and his teacher welcomed him. Within one month he was a regular, happy member of the class, and his parents reported him to be a different boy at home.

From the examples quoted it can be seen how self-concept theory can often be a useful framework to the resolving of behaviour difficulties. An assumption is that in addition the teacher needs to be of high self-esteem to be able to withstand the stresses involved in coping with behavioural difficulties. That topic is discussed in Chapter 12.

■ FURTHER READING ■

Charles, C. (1995) *Building Classroom Discipline*, Harlow, Longman.

Gray, P., Miller, A. and Nockes, J. (eds) (1994) *Challenging Behaviour in Schools*, London, Routledge.

Haigh, G. (1994) *Managing Classroom Problems in the Primary School*, London, Paul Chapman Publishing.

Merrett, F. and Wheldall, K. (1990) *Positive Teaching in the Primary School*, London, Paul Chapman Publishing.

Self-esteem and reading difficulties

Progress in reading attainment in children is dependent mainly on the quality of the teaching methods employed and the level of the child's language development. Most children learn to read well as a result of the dedicated professionalism of teachers. However, there is usually a small group of children in any school that finds the reading process difficult.

This group of children has received much attention from the researchers over the years with the aim of seeking the best method of helping them. This kind of research has focused on teaching the cognitive skills involved in the reading process. An example of this is the current emphasis on teaching phonological skills (Snowling, 1995). This 'skills approach' to teaching is not meant to imply that teachers ignore the affective state of children. Most teachers would ensure that the child is properly motivated and relaxed in order to benefit from their teaching. The child's self-esteem level is also usually recognized as an important factor in the child's progress.

> COGNITIVE SKILLS. This refers to the learning of skills that are concerned with thinking and problem-solving.

The research evidence indicting a correlation between self-esteem and achievement is well documented in the literature (Chapman and Tunmer, 2003; Galbraith and Alexander, 2005). However, the literature related to teaching reading is scant in its references to the need to incorporate a structured programme of self-esteem enhancement. This chapter shows why there is a need in some children to incorporate this kind of programme.

The research outlined in the Appendix gives the details of research conducted by the author that supports the need to focus on self-esteem when helping children improve their reading attainment. This research followed several years of working in psychological and remedial departments, and began as an investigation into possible differences between children who score highly on reading tests and those who were at least two years behind on the same tests.

It was hypothesized that there would be differences in personal adjustment. The Cattell personality questionnaire was administered to a random sample of good readers and also to a random sample of poor readers. A statistical significance was observed between the two groups on the 'O' factor which Cattell describes as 'the extent to which the individual feels guilty about himself … it is a crude measure of self-image' (Lawrence, 1971).

■ RESEARCH FINDINGS ■

As a result of this finding the experiments described were set up with the hypothesis that childrens' reading attainment would rise if they could be helped to feel less guilty about themselves, that is, improve their self-esteem. This hypothesis was subsequently verified.

From these experiments it looked as if self-esteem was causative over attainments, and over the years different researchers have argued about which comes first. The present conclusion seems to be that the relationship between reading attainment and self-esteem is a reciprocal one, with each affecting the other. In practice, therefore, a dual approach should be used in most instances. In a small number of cases, however, it is not possible to help the child achieve success with a skill approach until he/she has had a change of self-concept. These children usually have low self-esteem and so do not believe that they are capable of improving. Consequently, they are not motivated to learn and do not choose to pick up books unless pressed to do so. For these children a period of self-esteem enhancement through various activities is required before going on to introduce reading skills.

It is significant that whatever the type of provision or the level of expertise of the teacher, the kind of help given usually differs from what the child has already been receiving only to the extent that it is possible to give more individual attention. There continues to be a direct attack on the reading skills.

When children continue to fail despite remedial provision, the teacher often assumes that he/she has also failed. He/she feels that he/she has failed to find the right method or the best materials. The search then begins for different materials and methods. The evidence suggests that the reason for the child's failure may be in his/her low level of self-esteem and that a primarily therapeutic approach might be more successful, although this approach is rarely, if ever, considered. Teachers may recognize the child's need for emotional attention as well as for the more obvious need to teach the skills of reading but, beyond providing an atmosphere of encouragement, there is rarely an attempt to focus attention specifically on the child's self-concept.

To concentrate on enhancing self-esteem would be an unusual occurrence to say the least. In my experience whenever it has been suggested that the teacher do this, the response has been one of surprise that a teacher might 'just talk' with the child when he/she so obviously needs to improve his/her reading skills.

The comment has been made that the head of the school would be upset if they 'merely chatted' with these children instead of teaching them. It is sad that the view still seems to be prevalent amongst many educational administrators as well as amongst some teachers that teaching is all about the purveying of knowledge. The fact that teachers have a grave responsibility for the development of the personalities of the children in their care seems to escape many of them. The view has sometimes been expressed to me that the home is the place for emotional development and the school for learning skills.

The results of the investigation reported in this book would suggest that teachers could do both – enhance self-esteem and improve reading skills. It is somewhat daunting, however, to reflect on the fact that almost 50 years ago previous research was suggesting similar things, that is, that teachers who make warm accepting relationships with their pupils, avoiding negative and sarcastic comments, are those who in turn influence pupils' personality and attainments most (Perkins, 1958; Staines, 1958). Yet, 50 years on, many teachers still fail to appreciate the full significance of this kind of relationship.

There is still the tendency to demand more effort from the failing child when reference to the work of psychologists such as Rogers (1951) might help them to appreciate that sometimes the children who are failing in reading and seem to be avoiding it may be behaving simply according to their perception of themselves. In terms of Rogerian theory, behaviour is the goal-directed attempt of the organism to satisfy its needs as it is perceived in the field.

In the case of failing children, they see themselves as non-readers and so tend to avoid reading matter according to their perception of themselves. Whilst the teacher may see them as *potentially improving* readers, they see themselves as *permanently failed* readers. Their perception of themselves as failing readers has become part of their 'internal frame of reference' (Rogers, 1951).

MOTIVATION AND REINFORCEMENT

It is clear from the work of Rogers and others in the phenomenological schools of psychology that the self-concept is a motivator. People tend to behave in ways which fit in with their perceptions of themselves. This is discussed further in Chapter 1. Those teachers who ignore self-concept theory will continue to focus on the pure skills approach and will continue to find some children who do not make progress. The view has been expressed that all children can learn by breaking down the material to be learned into sufficiently small units and providing suitable reinforcement of behaviour (Skinner, 1953). In my experience, and that of several remedial colleagues in practice, it is not always possible to do this. In the first place some children are not attracted to any obvious reinforcer. It becomes impossible, therefore, to get these children on the first rung of that ladder of success.

Even when it may be possible to find a suitable reinforcer and learning does take place, these children do not always retain the material for very long. This can be so baffling to the teacher and there is a tendency to dismiss it with the explanation that the child has a 'poor memory'. A more likely explanation could lie within the *locus of control* construct which is discussed in Chapter 8. According to this view, the child would need to believe that his/her own action was instrumental in receiving the reinforcer (Rotter, 1954). Those designated as 'externally controlled' do not believe that they are responsible for what happens to them. In other words, there is evidence from the work in the locus of control area that a reinforcer may not be sufficient in itself to produce a change in behaviour which lasts.

THERAPEUTIC APPROACHES

For many children retarded in reading, a concentration early in the programme on reading skills gives confidence as they do indeed learn. These are the children whose reading difficulties are not usually of long standing and are not usually associated with any serious emotional problems. Quick success for them soon sets up the happy circle of improved reading and self-esteem (Figure 11.1).

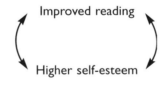

Improved reading

Higher self-esteem

Figure 11.1 *The happy circle*

To organize a therapeutic approach for these children might produce an enjoyable experience for them, but it might be seen as wasting valuable time and resources which could be spent more profitably on children more obviously in need of therapy.

The problem of deciding which are the children in need of therapy and which do not need it should be resolved, ideally, during an initial diagnosis before treatment begins. However, it would be a costly exercise to refer all cases of reading difficulties to a specialist such as an educational psychologist. Perhaps this is one reason why education departments usually operate on the principle that the majority of failing readers will respond to a skills approach, with a remedial teacher providing the necessary input.

It is only when these children do not respond to this approach that an educational psychologist would be asked to see the child. Normally this would be the first attempt to investigate possible emotional causes of the reading failure. A planned programme of help would be drawn up on the basis of this investigation which may involve both parents and children in therapy. Although at this stage there is recognition that emotional factors may have an important part to play in the problem, it would be rare for the recommendation for treatment to involve a self-esteem enhancement approach. In my experience this has never happened.

There continues to be an emphasis on the skill acquisition usually through the organization of a more structured programme often with operant conditioning as its basis. The possible emotional factors receive attention through regular meetings between the child and the psychologist, with the aim of helping the child resolve possible emotional conflicts or anxieties. Whilst in some cases this can be an effective means of helping, it is time-consuming, costly and, more important from the child's point of view, perhaps not even necessary.

There are less costly and perhaps more effective ways of helping most children retarded in reading. This would involve the establishment of a therapeutic programme in the school for the purpose of self-esteem enhancement. Only those children who did not respond to this programme would need the more skilled help of the educational psychologist. Although the experimental results clearly support the philosophy of therapeutic treatment, which treatment to use depends on the organization of the school as well as on the children.

For instance, the results suggest that some children do better through drama than through an individual self-esteem enhancement programme.

The original research had a drama group in addition to the individual pro-gramme. The drama group used some of the activities outlined in Chapters 7 and 8. Those children initially of lower self-esteem would appear to ben-efit more through drama, whilst those of initially higher self-esteem would appear to respond slightly better to an individual programme. Although the lower self-esteem children do slightly better with drama than with the individual approach the effects of the difference between these treatments were small. In practice, therefore, it might be more expedient to apply the therapeutic approaches suggested in Chapters 7 and 8 to most children. It would be sensible to do this for all the children who had not made progress with the usual skills approach.

There may be times when it would not be worth the expense and effort to organize a self-esteem enhancement programme, particularly if the school already has an emphasis on drama in the normal curriculum. Only the particular self-esteem orientation and perhaps the content of the drama would need to be specially organized. In other words, the choice of a self-esteem enhancement programme or drama as a therapeutic treat-ment would depend mainly on the exigencies of the school concerned.

The results of the experiment suggest additional advantages which accrue from the different treatments in terms of enhanced self-esteem and a shift towards internality on the locus of control dimension. However, it was reading attainment which was the main focus of attention in these experiments and which presumably would also be the main focus of atten-tion for the remedial teacher.

■ SELECTING APPROPRIATE TREATMENT FOR READING PROGRAMMES ■

Although the decision over which treatment to apply in a given case will depend mainly as stated on the school involved, it is important to empha-size that it should match the child. As an aid to this matching process the sequence model in Figure 11.2, based on the results of the main experi-ment, is suggested.

To understand the model it would help teachers to be aware of the

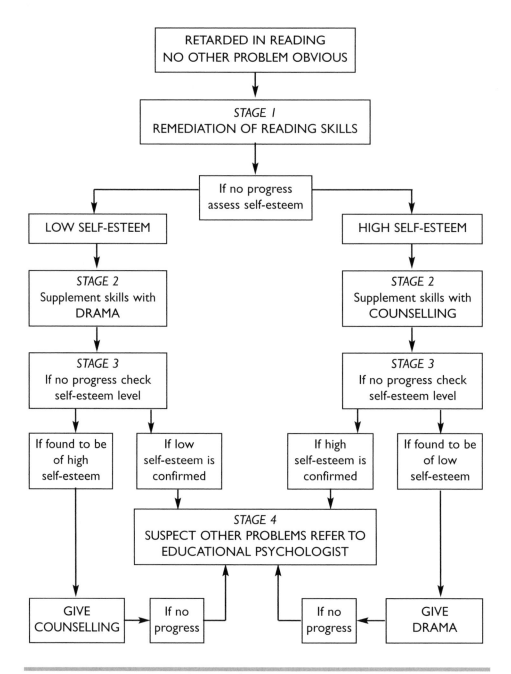

Figure 11.2 *Processing sequence for retarded readers*

different categories into which failing readers fall. A child may have a difficulty in one or several of these areas. Assuming that there are no obvious physical or sensory disabilities four stages of processing are recommended.

STAGE 1

Stage 1 would show a concentration on remediating skills of reading, and it is hypothesized that the majority of failing readers would be helped at this stage. They would be children whose reading difficulties are not of long standing and are not normally associated with other problems. These children usually achieve quick success as discussed earlier. Those who do not respond to this treatment would fall into Stage 2.

STAGE 2

At Stage 2, those children who made no progress using the pure skills approach of Stage 1 should receive therapeutic treatment in addition to further help with reading skills. It is suggested that an individual self-esteem enhancement programme be organized for the low self-esteem children as was used successfully in the main experiment. Drama should be used if the children have been identified as of particularly low self-esteem. However, as discussed earlier, the type of therapeutic treatment – a full self-esteem enhancement programme or drama – would depend largely on the exigencies of the school.

STAGE 3

Stage 3 would be for those children remaining who have not made progress despite having gone through the previous stages. They would require further investigation into their level of self-esteem as some might easily be those referred to, by Byrne (1961), as 'repressors'. In other words, those who had seemed to be of high self-esteem may have been repressing their 'true' self-esteem and would really be of low self-esteem. If, indeed, they had been repressing their low self-esteem and were really of high self-esteem, then they should be given drama. There may also be children in this group who were wrongly assessed as being of high self-esteem. These children should be given the self-esteem enhancement programme.

STAGE 4

Stage 4 would be concerned with those children who have not responded well to any of the other approaches. They would be in a small minority and should be referred to an educational psychologist for a more skilled assessment and treatment. Those with severe emotional and social difficulties and/or possible physical or sensory difficulties would come into this category. It is likely that they would be showing overt signs of their emotional difficulties through challenging behaviour in the classroom.

It is Stage 3 which is the focus of interest with its processing of therapeutic treatments, and for which the experimental results provided evidence.

■ THE MAINTENANCE OF READING GAINS IN THE LONG TERM ■

The question of the effectiveness of remedial education has over the years proved to be a controversial issue. There have been those who have written of its undoubted value and also those who have cast doubt on its long-term effectiveness (Collins, 1961; Chazan, 1967; Cashdan and Pumfrey, 1969). This is debated at some length in the Bullock Report (1975) which points out the conflicting evidence and the difficulties involved in evaluating the various remedial provision.

Remedial education means different things to different workers; the criteria for selecting the children are variable and types of provision vary between education authorities. Despite this difficulty of being able to evaluate the remedial work, writers continue to argue over its effectiveness. Whatever the conclusions it is interesting and significant to note that the research is notable for its lack of attention to the self-concept.

It is strongly advocated here that, before conclusions are drawn with any real validity, attempts should have been made in the research to focus on the child's self-concept, and it is suggested that long-term gains would be made only where there has been a corresponding change in the self-concept. It is only through a change in the child's perception of him/herself that the he/she will begin to perceive him/herself as a good reader. Therefore, only with this will come the motivation to seek out reading matter independently and in so doing rehearse what has been learned. Without this corresponding change in the self-concept the child will merely have learned to perform a few tricks with words. The motivation to seek out further reading will not be there. He/she will continue with his/her former attitudes towards reading and have the attitude that 'it is not me'. Once able to perceive him/herself differently he/she will be more inclined to seek further reading experiences outside the remedial lesson.

Without a change of self-concept, any improvements made during remedial lessons are not necessarily perceived as significant to the child – as part of his/her self-concept. Although having pleased the teacher by learning additional skills, away from the teacher these children continue to perceive themselves as poor readers and will quickly revert to their former state of reading inadequacy. So it is not surprising to discover in various studies that long-term gains are negligible.

■ THE EFFECTS OF THERAPEUTIC INTERVENTION ON DYSLEXIC CHILDREN ■

Dyslexia is a term used to describe children who have a specific difficulty in learning literacy skills, as opposed to those who are seen to have an all-round general learning difficulty. Arguments over the usefulness of this term continue to fill the pages of journals and books. There are those on the one hand who deny the concept altogether, whilst at the other extreme there are those who stoutly maintain that there is a group of children who have specific learning difficulties, usually in the area of working memory, which require specialist help. Most researchers in this area would concur with the view that some children indeed do have specific learning difficulties which inevitably cause them problems in learning to read and to spell properly.

It is interesting that in the experiments described in the Appendix no attempt was made to screen children for dyslexia. Surveys of the numbers of children who could be considered to fall into the dyslexic category vary from 4 per cent in British surveys (Miles and Haslum, 1986) to 25 per cent in American surveys (Farnham and Diggory, 1978). If one accepts these figures, undoubtedly there would have been a considerable number of dyslexic children amongst those in the experimental groups. Some of these children may have contributed to the 'within group' errors. Any dyslexic children presumably would have been distributed randomly over the four treatment groups and, if they had been excluded from the final statistical analysis, it is probable that the differences between the treatments would have been even more marked.

Children with specific learning difficulties, known as dyslexia, are likely to present a special case of low self-esteem unless identified early. The research would suggest that a specific learning difficulty of this sort can last throughout life and without a thorough psychological assessment teachers are not going to know how best to help the children cope with the problems and perhaps how to compensate for them. Low self-esteem can soon develop under these circumstances.

The bright child who has not had a cognitive assessment identifying the precise nature of his/her difficulties would experience particular frustration. This child is often well able to contribute intelligently in oral lessons, easily capable of understanding the import of the discussion but unable to read or write about it without some considerable effort. Anthony (1968), in a study of children with symptoms of dyslexia, referred to a 'global stress' factor which he described as limiting the children's capacity to cope.

Whilst this observation would probably apply not only to dyslexics but also to most children with learning difficulties, once again it highlights the relationship between low self-esteem and literacy skills. Children who feel unable to cope are certainly at risk of developing low self-esteem.

It is possible that the extent to which a learning disability results in a handicapping condition depends on the level of self-esteem. Some children who are dyslexic may have learned to cope and so maintain their self-esteem by concentrating on their strengths. An accurate cognitive profile identifying strengths and weaknesses in the child is essential in knowing how best to teach children with reading difficulties, whether categorized as dyslexic or otherwise.

■ FURTHER READING ■

Brown E.N. (1990) Children with spelling and writing difficulties: an alternative approach, in P. Pumphrey and C. Elliott (eds) *Children's Difficulties in Reading, Spelling and Writing*, Lewes, Falmer.

Bryant, P. and Bradley, L. (1985) *Children's Reading Problems*, Oxford, Blackwell.

Chapman, J.W. and Tunmer, W.E. (2003) Reading difficulties, reading related self-perceptions, and strategies for overcoming negative self-beliefs, *Reading and Writing Quarterly*, 19, pp. 5–24.

Edwards, J. (1994) *The Scars of Dyslexia*, London, Cassell.

Hanko, G. (1985) *Special Needs in Ordinary Classrooms: Supporting Teachers*, Oxford, Blackwell.

Miles, T. and Miles, E. (1999) *Dyslexia: One Hundred Years On*, 2nd edn, Milton Keynes, Open University Press.

Lawrence, D. (1973) *Improved Reading Through Counselling*, London, Ward Lock.

Pumphrey, P.D. and Reason, R. (1991) *Specific Learning Difficulties (Dyslexia), Challenges and Responses*, Windsor, NFER-Nelson.

Wattenburg, W. and Clifford, C. (1964) Relation of self-concepts to beginning achievement in reading, *Child Development*, 35, pp. 461–7.

The teacher's self-esteem

There is clear evidence to show that without teachers themselves being confident and having high self-esteem they are not easily going to be able to enhance the self-esteem of the children in their care. So what can teachers do to ensure their own high self-esteem?

The bookstalls and popular press have always had 'experts' of one kind or another giving advice on how to 'feel more confident', how to 'lead a fuller life', how to 'feel in control of your life', and so on. The trouble with popular advice of this kind is that it is rarely based on sound theory and research. To enhance your own self-esteem it is desirable, first, to be aware of the theoretical background of self-concept, as outlined in earlier chapters. Secondly, it requires a belief in the hedonistic philosophy, which may be difficult for some teachers to accept. Thirdly, it requires commitment to the belief that we all have the power for change within ourselves. This means that we are potentially capable of being self-determinate, often despite unfortunate past life events. Finally, it means being able to accept and value the 'inner self' and to be able to distinguish it from the 'outward behaviour'.

Each of these principles of self-esteem enhancement will be discussed. The reader will have become familiar with self-concept theory having read the earlier chapters. The second principle of the self-esteem enhancement for the teacher is the acceptance of the hedonistic philosophy.

THE HEDONISTIC PHILOSOPHY

There are probably more philosophies of life than there are theories in psychology, the most common being those of a religious flavour and concerned with giving help to others. However, one important aspect of these philosophies of helping others, which tends to receive scant attention, is that before we can effectively have regard for others we need to have regard for ourselves. The phrase 'Charity begins at home' is so apt here. We are more likely to like others if we first like ourselves. Unfortunately, liking yourself is not always easy especially once the low self-esteem process has begun. Also, the view is sometimes expressed that giving too much attention to our own needs is selfish and therefore undesirable.

The hedonistic philosophy implies that giving expression to our own needs is essential to self-esteem enhancement, but this does not mean expressing them with no regard for the feelings of others. It emphasizes the social nature of humanity. It emphasizes that life is meant to be enjoyed and does not agree with the view that goodness only exists through denial. It means that we should take stock of our lifestyle and ask whether we are receiving job satisfaction.

Teaching is inherently demanding and job satisfaction can quickly be reduced through factors such as role ambiguity, difficult staff relations and coping with difficult children. All these have been identified by researchers as common sources of stress in teaching (Pratt, 1978). Job overload and role ambiguity have increased over the past two decades as countless changes in education have been introduced in schools. This has resulted in an inevitable rise in teacher stress. Prolonged stress and reduced job satisfaction will produce feelings of inadequacy, and therefore low self-esteem, in the teacher. Sources of stress such as those identified as common should be removed as far as possible before they result in low self-esteem.

If a teacher is not enjoying school then efforts should be made to identify the reasons for this and so remove the barriers to satisfaction. It is not justified to adopt the view that teaching has inevitably to be stressful or that it is 'character-building' to suffer stress. Although there will be aspects of school life which are sometimes unpleasant, they should not be accepted as inevitable. A hedonistic philosophy does not mean an acceptance of adverse circumstances. It is an active philosophy which focuses on the need to work at producing a more enjoyable lifestyle.

There are some sources of stress in teaching which are not always within the power of the teacher to change, for example, the relationship with the school head and the administration. Providing, however, that the teacher controls those factors which are controllable and has begun to develop high self-esteem these other factors will cease to have potency. High self-esteem in all of us has the effect of increasing our coping capacities.

The question is, 'How can the teacher set about developing high self-esteem and so increase his/her capacity to cope with the inevitable stressors of change?' The evidence from clinical work, and from the humanistic school of psychology in particular, shows that it is perfectly possible for people to change their behaviour and their emotions if they are sufficiently motivated and prepared to make the necessary effort to do so. The remainder of this chapter is devoted to showing teachers how to maintain their self-esteem and so reduce the effects of stress.

■ CHANGING EMOTIONS BY CHANGING THINKING ■

It is a mistake to think that we are all prisoners of our early experiences. The classical Freudian view implies that our inadequacies are so often relics of our childhood days and to remove their effects it is necessary to relive these early experiences. It is now generally accepted that this view is extreme and that it is possible to resolve present difficulties and to change present attitudes without always needing to 'unravel the past'. The evidence points to the view that people are motivated not only by their past experiences but also by their anticipation of the future. We are all capable of change if we wish to do so and are prepared for the effort. How do we set about doing this?

Events themselves do not cause emotions. Emotions are caused by our interpretation of events. Following this line of reasoning it becomes clear that it is possible to change emotions by thinking in a particular way. This 'rational-emotive' approach to behaviour forms the basis of the theories of Albert Ellis (1979). Although his theories are more usually encountered in psychotherapy, they also have something to offer teachers and others who may find themselves under stress. The following scene illustrates this and describes the steps to go through when setting out to reduce stress by changing thinking.

SCENE

A teacher feels inadequate because of regularly troublesome behaviour of two pupils in her class. These pupils disrupt lessons and seem impervious to any approach. The teacher goes home at the end of each day exhausted and with feelings of failure.

STRATEGY

The situation should be clearly analysed under the three headings of 'thinking–feeling–action'.

Step 1: Analysis of feelings at time of stress. Possible answer: 'I felt angry, silly and humiliated.'

Step 2: Analysis of thinking at time of stress. Possible answer: 'I am no good as a teacher. The children do not like me.' This step is often difficult for people. They may say, 'I wasn't thinking of anything. I was too angry at the time'. The very fact of being forced to trace the origins of the emotions and to be able to put these emotions into words is the essence of the rational-emotive approach. So, no matter how difficult it may seem, it is important that the thinking is recalled and analysed.

Step 3: Analysis of behaviour at the time of the stress. Possible answer: 'I shouted and clenched my fists.'

Step 4: Go through the following relaxation procedure:

■ Sit in a comfortable chair which supports your head.

- Focus on a point on the ceiling until your eyes become tired and begin to blink.

- Close your eyes as it becomes unpleasant to leave them open.

- Think of each muscle and joint in your body in turn, beginning with the ankles.

- Whilst doing this say the word 'relax' as you move to the next one.

- Focus particularly on your stomach muscles.

- Conclude by relaxing your facial muscles and even the tongue.

- Now observe your breathing, remembering that it is automatic.

- Let 'it' breathe as and when 'it' wants to.

- With every breath out say the word 'relax'.

- Repeat this ten times.

Step 5: Visualize yourself as a successful teacher, smiling and with a happy contented class. See in your mind's eye the troublesome pupils and visualize them behaving properly. Talk to yourself, saying positive things about yourself changing those words used when under stress and substituting them for positive ones, for example, 'I get on well with the other pupils and they like me. I know I am becoming a better teacher every day'. It is important to visualize the scene in addition to changing your thinking, as the aim is to 'condition the unconscious mind' which operates in pictures.

Step 6: Deliberately seek out the stressful situation in real life and as soon as the feelings of stress make their appearance say quietly to yourself the word 'relax'. Immediately the body will begin to assume a relaxed mode. On the first occasion after having gone through the procedure only a slight change will be experienced. With regular practice, however, a permanent change will occur. The relaxation and visualization should be practised once a day until the situation is no longer felt to be stressful. This would normally take no longer than a fortnight.

Another example of a stressful teacher could be someone who worries over not getting on with other teachers in the staffroom. This is common, as the research into sources of teacher stress indicates. The teacher would need to translate this worry into specific behaviour and as a result may discover that other teachers do not talk to him/her very much. The next step would be to ask him/herself why this is so. The answer invariably would be that there is something wrong with the others. Whilst this may be so, to blame others does not solve the problem.

The teacher must always ask him/herself 'What is it in me that results in this behaviour?' The answer could be that the teacher has developed the habit now of avoiding or ignoring social contact. In that case, the desired behaviour change would be to practise making friendly overtures and initiating conversations. The teacher may say 'He/she made me angry'. This is not the case in actual fact. The teacher made him/herself angry.

THINK POSITIVE

It is all too easy for teachers to fall into the habit of negative thinking, particularly if they have to deal with difficult behaviour in children. They also tend to be unduly critical of themselves and blame themselves for not being able to deal with the behaviour. An interesting experiment was devised by Hannum (1974) to help teachers become less critical.

Hannum set out to help two teachers become less self-critical. The aim was to increase their positive thoughts about themselves and to decrease their negative self-thoughts. They were asked to count their thoughts on a wrist-band counter and observers in the classroom noted their negative and positive behaviours towards the students. Following a baseline period, they were asked deliberately to say 'stop' whenever they felt a negative thought coming on. There was a gradual increase in positive thoughts and also in positive behaviour towards the students. All that was required was for the teachers to make a conscious effort to change their negative set.

▇ SELF-ACCEPTANCE ▇

The required changes in our emotions and subsequently in behaviour do not always occur immediately and need regular practice. In the meantime, it is essential that the teacher accepts the undesirable behaviour in him/herself until the changes are felt. This is where the principle of self-acceptance is important. This requires an attitude of acceptance of the possibility of change as discussed but, in addition, requires the ability to separate our behaviour from our 'inner self'. It is likely to need practice as changes are being attempted from behaviour which is probably of long standing, and habit is a strong motivating factor in all behaviours. Self-acceptance is similar to the principle, discussed in Chapter 6, of accepting the personality of the child even if not accepting the child's behaviour.

A first step towards this self-acceptance is the process of affirmation. The following affirmations should be practised:

- 'I am a confident person.'
- 'I am a strong person.'
- 'I am a happy person.'
- 'My motives are always for the best.'
- 'I am improving in every way.'

Acceptance of inadequacies and/or failures should be practised by affirming the preceding and recognizing that, even when the behaviour is sometimes not exactly what was desired or planned, the inner self is still intact and is 'doing its best'. It is particularly important that this kind of attitude is practised following an unpleasant experience which may have resulted in feelings of inadequacy. Implicit in this affirmation is the belief in the separateness of the self.

We often tell ourselves 'we are no good' when we have had a personal failure. This statement is made when we have not separated our behaviour from our unique inner self. Once we can make this distinction we can appreciate the illogicality of saying 'I am no good' as a result of one unpleasant situation. We should say instead, 'My behaviour was no good but I am still a strong, confident, happy person inside'. Next time perhaps the behaviour will not be so bad.

In other words, 'I like me even if I sometimes dislike what I do'. The adoption of this attitude will prevent the low self-esteem person from continually punishing him/herself and feeling guilty.

■ CHALLENGING PARENTS AS A THREAT TO SELF-ESTEEM ■

Regular practice of the preceding principles should help reduce stress and so maintain the teacher's self-esteem but, in addition, it is also helpful to be prepared for situations which can be a threat to self-esteem. Amongst these are parents who are a challenge to the teacher's professionalism.

The chances are high that most teachers sooner or later will encounter this situation. Usually this is as a result of an invitation from the teacher to discuss the child's behaviour or work. Less frequently, it will be as a result of a parent arriving at the school, often unannounced, to complain about the school's treatment of his/her child. Whether the parent arrives on his/her own initiative or by invitation, the situation is fraught with the potential for further difficulties. Whether or not these further difficulties subsequently appear is largely going to depend on the skill of the teacher in the area of interpersonal relationships.

COPING WITH CONFRONTATIONAL PARENTS

The starting point for coping with this situation is to try to see the parent's point of view. This means recognizing first that if the parent is there because of difficulties with the child, he/she is likely to feel inadequate and be on the defensive.

The manner in which parents of a child will protect their self-esteem will vary along a continuum ranging from overtly aggressive to timid, withdrawn behaviour. Which is shown depends on the parent's temperament. It seems that those more extroverted by temperament are inclined to be aggressive, whilst the more introverted in temperament are likely to be withdrawn and nervous. From the teacher's point of view, it is useful to know that whichever behaviour is shown, the chances are that it is an attempt to maintain self-esteem in the face of feelings of possible sorrow and inadequacy. Once this is understood, the teacher is less likely to react with irritation or aggression, and so remains able to establish productive communication.

As a prelude to discussing the nature of the child's problem it is essential that the parent is helped to appreciate that the interview is non-threatening to his/her self-esteem. Once this has been communicated the inter-view should begin by inviting the parent to take a seat and by sitting along-side him/her without the barrier of a desk. The psychology of non-verbal behaviour tells us that an interview conducted from behind a desk conveys a message of superiority. As a further prelude, it is important to regard the problem as a 'problem situation' and not a 'problem child' or a 'problem parent'.

The aim should be not to apportion blame, but rather for teacher and parent to work together to try to resolve the difficult situation. Unfortunately, it is not enough to have this intention. Even when parents accept that the teacher is not an active threat to their self-esteem, they are still likely to find, on occasions, that they cannot get 'on the teacher's wave-length'. We have all had the experience of feeling that we are not being understood and, in the case of a confrontational parent, it is essential for the teacher to be able to establish an empathic relationship. If this kind of relationship can be established quickly, the parent is more likely to trust the teacher and therefore to be more receptive to suggestions of change. Unfortunately, empathy is not always easy to achieve.

Obviously, it will be easier if the parent and teacher come from simi-lar backgrounds. The more alike they are the more they will understand the other's point of view. This is just the beginning of the establishment of an empathic relationship. Equally important is the ability to listen.

Listening means more than just hearing verbal utterances. It means also, in this context, being able to hear the feelings behind the words. This is a skill many people seem to possess naturally, but it can always be trained. It involves being able to reflect the feelings once they have been perceived, for example, if the parent should say 'I don't know what to do to make my son work', the teacher should try to understand what the par-ent is feeling when the statement is made. It is possible for many feelings to be expressed. If the feeling seems to be 'I feel helpless' then the teacher might reflect this feeling, for example, 'You sound as if you feel helpless in this situation'.

In addition to the reflection of feeling, another skill as an aid to empa-thy is the capacity for revealing one's own personality. It helps, for instance, if the teacher can communicate that he/she has met that problem before:

'I know what you mean, my child was the same.' So much the better, of course, if this can be followed up with a comment that eventually the difficulties were resolved.

In summary, the following sequence of events should be followed:

1. Welcome the parent and communicate acceptance.
2. Allow the parent time to express his/her feelings without criticism.
3. Emphasize the 'problem situation' and not the 'problem child'.
4. Try to show genuineness and empathy throughout the interview.

DEALING WITH THREATS TO TEACHERS' PROFESSIONALISM

So far we have looked at the confrontational parent. A slightly different problem is the parent who complains that his/her child is not achieving as highly as he/she wishes. It is important that the same principles as already discussed are maintained, but in this case it is easier for the teacher to begin to feel inadequate. To be accused by an articulate parent of being a poor teacher is almost calculated to result in feelings of aggression, or in feelings of insecurity and inadequacy in the teacher. However, if the teacher is prepared for this reaction he/she will handle it better.

If teachers recognize that any professional is at risk in this way, then they will not overreact. The question is: why should teachers feel threatened by such accusations? In the first place, we all need to be liked and to receive approval. If our competence is threatened our immediate reaction is normally to feel disappointment. This feeling is then usually replaced by indignation. It may stop there, particularly if the teacher knows that the parent's accusations are unfounded. However, it is not always easy in education to be sure that what we do is always responsible for the outcomes. More often than not, therefore, the teacher who is unprepared is going to be prey to undesirable emotions. What can be done about them?

A strong self-concept is more likely to be able to cope with these feelings; this means a person who is doing a satisfying job and is confident that he/she is doing it well. A strong self-concept means being able to communicate easily and to be spontaneous in emotional expression. It means, above all, having a knowledge of one's own personality. This means that when feelings of irritation or feelings of insecurity ensue, reason will prevail. It will be possible to listen to the parent's criticisms objectively without overreacting. Unfortunately, not all of us have this kind of strength.

For most of us, perhaps, an attack on our professional competence is a potential threat to our self-esteem. Once we experience this threat we should immediately ask ourselves, 'What is it in me which causes me to feel like this?' This question will have the main purpose of reminding the teacher that the feeling indeed originates from within and is not something imposed by the parent. It will also have the purpose of causing the teacher to think before acting adversely. It is a bit like 'counting to ten' before saying something when angry. It should then be possible to begin the negotiation with the relationship still intact and without the teacher feeling loss of self-esteem.

Teachers who recognize their lack of assertion need not be discouraged as there is plenty of evidence to illustrate that with practice they can become gradually more assertive. The key phrase here is 'with practice'. The importance of being prepared cannot be overemphasized, so that the very words to be used have been rehearsed. Thomas Gordon (1974) has shown how the use of the three words 'I', 'when' and 'because' are the key to successful communication in this context. Although Gordon was advocating using this formula with children, the same principles apply when communicating assertively with another adult. The following sentences illustrate:

- ■ 'I feel upset when people do that because I cannot hear myself speak.'
- ■ 'I feel angry when I'm interrupted because it seems that my opinion does not count.'
- ■ 'I become embarrassed when asked to do that because I feel undervalued.'

The main points are that feelings are communicated without fear and that a reason for them is given.

BE ORGANIZED

Insecurities and stress can come from not having planned the day properly. Teachers know full well the importance of planning lessons but how many have made a plan for the whole day, including after school? It seems to be a natural phenomenon for human beings to 'know where they stand'. Nature abhors a vacuum and it is a source of comfort to know what is to be expected. Ambiguities are a common source of stress. It is suggested that teachers begin each day with the motto: 'Plan for the day', not just 'Plan for the teaching'.

Plan for the day

- Make a list of 'jobs for the day' in order of their importance.
- Estimate the time required for each job.
- Plan a few minutes of personal relaxation during the day.
- Make a list of 'jobs for the term'.
- Plan for privacy if necessary, for example, close the door and place on it 'Do Not Disturb'.
- Delegate jobs where possible.
- Spend five minutes just thinking about the role of a teacher.

BECOME AN EXPERT

The world seems to need experts. This is probably a reflection of the times in which we live. So if a teacher can develop a talent through a particular interest it usually has the effect of enhancing self-esteem as others notice the talent and admire it. The fascinating thing is that you do not need to be a real expert in the true sense of the word for this to happen, so great is the need for people to admire experts. Simply developing a reputation for being interested in a particular area, for example, dyslexia, will cause others to regard you as the expert. This will cause the teacher's self-image to be changed and as the self is a motivator this regard from others will cause the teacher to seek out information on dyslexia. Very soon the teacher will begin to know more about the subject than his/her colleagues. The lesson is for teachers to take an interest in a specialist area.

■ HAVE FUN ■

Teaching can be a very serious job if we let it be so. It is not always easy to be lighthearted in the face of all the stresses which go with the job. The other side of the coin is that people who have a sense of humour and appear to have fun in their work usually have high self-esteem. So teachers should ensure that they maintain their sense of humour and deliberately ensure they do have fun when that is possible. By all means take your work seriously, but never take yourself seriously to the extent that you lose your sense of humour! The lesson for us all is that we have to set about organizing our lives so that we have a regular period set aside for having fun, whether this be a night out in a restaurant or a night in watching a favourite television programme.

■ MAINTAINING SELF-ESTEEM AS A MANAGER ■

The management of a team in any organization should be based on sound management principles. Whilst this is a topic in its own right, and one which can only be dealt with superficially at the risk of trivializing it, there is one aspect of team management which has to be addressed here. This is the problem of maintaining self-esteem whilst managing a team of teachers. Teachers are a group of professionals renowned for their individualism, and managing them can present some considerable problems.

In general terms there are broadly three different styles of leadership – the laissez-faire type, where the leader is content to allow decisions to be made according to the whims of the group, the authoritarian, where the leader makes decisions without consulting the group and, finally, the democratic leader, where decisions are made with group consultation. Not surprisingly, it is the democratic style of leadership which is judged to be the most effective in maintaining self-esteem and group morale. The other two leadership styles, as well as being bad for group morale, also tend to produce hostility in a group.

In Chapter 6 mention was made of those desirable qualities of personality which make for effective communicators – empathy, genuineness and acceptance. These same qualities, of course, are essential in a team manager. They are particularly important when the manager has to make demands on others, which the others may have difficulty in accepting. The democratic manager who possesses these qualities will also have high self-esteem and be able to be assertive. Demands will then be made through a process of negotiation using 'I' messages and active listening (empathy) as illustrated in the following dramatic scene. This formula can also be considered as a four-step method for resolving conflict as follows:

- *Step 1*: Both parties express their needs using active listening with 'I' messages.
- *Step 2*: Active listening (empathy) is used to consider possible solutions.
- *Step 3*: Alternative solutions are then considered without criticism.
- *Step 4*: A solution is agreed upon through consensus, so nobody loses.

RESOLVING CONFLICTS: A FOUR-STEP METHOD

- *Step 1*: Both parties express their needs. Active listening is used along with 'I' messages.
- *Step 2*: Possible solutions are considered and active listening continues to be used.
- *Step 3*: Alternative solutions are considered without criticism.
- *Step 4*: A solution is adopted through consensus so nobody loses.

Example

The headteacher has sent a note to the school caretaker asking him to prepare a room in the school and to have it open next Saturday for the first meeting of the school chess club. The caretaker has said that he cannot do this owing to another commitment. They meet.

Headteacher	I need the room prepared with adequate seating and to be open by 9 a.m. on Saturday because Saturdays are the only time we can get the students and their parents together ['I' messages].
Caretaker	I can't do it on Saturday. I have a family, you know.
Headteacher	It sounds as if you have made arrangements which are difficult to break [empathy].
Caretaker	Yes, I have, I've promised them I'd go camping with them next Saturday so I can't help.
Headteacher	You probably feel you would be letting them down if you had to cancel the camp. Is there any way around this do you think? [Step 2.]
Caretaker	Well, why not have the chess group during the week?
Headteacher	That sounds a good idea but the parents won't all be able to come during the week. How would it be if we had the meeting the following Saturday? [Step 3.]
Caretaker	I think I could manage that but I'd have to come back early from the camp.
Headteacher	OK. How about the Saturday after that one? [Step 4.]
Caretaker	Yes, that would be fine. No problems at all.

Example

The team manager has asked a particular teacher to take a group of school children along to a football match on a Saturday morning. Nobody wants to do this on their day off!

Manager	I need somebody to take the children to the game as I cannot go myself. They have all expressed disappointment at the thought of missing it and I do think they should see the game ['I' message].
Teacher	I can't go as I've promised to take my family to buy some new clothes this Saturday.
Manager	It sounds then as if you are already committed [empathy].
Teacher	Yes, I'm afraid so. They have to have new things for their holiday next month.

Manager	So you feel you would be letting them down if you had to cancel their shopping [empathy]. Is there any way around this, do you think? [Step 2.]
Teacher	Well, I could put the shopping off until another day but I just don't have the time, unless of course I could take some time off during school hours.
Manager	Taking time off sounds a possible solution but first have you thought of asking your husband to take your children shopping? [Step 3.]
Teacher	What! He is hopeless at that sort of thing. He would not know what to buy.
Manager	I see. Well supposing the head would agree to your taking time off, would that really be the answer to the problem?
Teacher	Well, yes, if the head agrees to my doing the shopping on Thursday morning then I could take the children to the game on Saturday as you have asked me to do.
Manager	Right! I'm sure the head would agree under the circumstances. [Step 4.]

Using the four-step method meant that there were no winners or losers in this conflict. The following principles were observed in this process:

- The manager made his needs known clearly by using 'I' messages.
- The teacher was given the opportunity to react to the messages.
- The manager used active listening, communicating understanding of the teacher's feelings.
- The teacher was given the opportunity to suggest possible solutions.
- A compromise solution was obtained through negotiation.

ACCEPT YOUR LIMITATIONS

Most teachers are known for being 'tender minded' and caring people. Whilst these are admirable qualities for people in the helping professions – and I would consider teaching to be a helping profession – they can place teachers at a disadvantage when having to cope with stress. An example of this is the common observation that teachers tend to blame themselves if the children in their care have problems. The teacher with the child who does not make progress in reading attainment asks him/herself why he/she cannot find the way through to help this child. The teacher with the child who is a discipline problem asks him/herself why he/she cannot control the class.

Whilst this kind of introspective self-examination can lead to constructive action, it can also become intropunitive and can generalize to the extent that the teacher ends up questioning his/her suitability for the job. It is important that teachers understand that all teachers are a prey to this kind of thinking and they need to be able to distance themselves from the child with the problem. With regard to academic attainments they should remind themselves that there will always be some children for whom progress is going to be slow.

In the case of behavioural difficulties, there will always be some children who are so emotionally disturbed that they cannot be helped in the ordinary classroom. Teachers should not be afraid to admit that they may have a child whom they cannot control. It is sometimes thought to be a character defect if a teacher cannot control children. This is wrong. It cannot be sufficiently emphasized that controlling groups of children can be very difficult and is a skill which has to be learned. There are many well-researched strategies which teachers can put into practice but teachers are not born knowing what they are! They need to be shown what to do! The first step is to accept they do have a problem in this area and then request help either from a senior colleague, the local educational psychologist or apply to go on an in-service course.

EXPRESSING PLEASURE AT SUCCESSES

Most teachers are modest people. This may be largely a cultural factor. People in our culture do not easily broadcast their achievements. Why should we not announce with pleasure in the staffroom that we have just been able to get a difficult child to read, or that we have just passed our latest examination? Perhaps it could be a routine procedure at the end of a staff meeting for the head to ask if anybody has any achievements or been known to have made a particular effort during the previous week they would like to announce. A refinement of this would be for the head to ask staff to let him/her know before the staff meeting of any teachers who have experienced a notable success or been known to have made a big effort in some direction. A tangible recognition of this could then be presented to the appropriate teacher at the meeting followed by a round of applause from the others.

IT IS OK TO CHANGE YOUR MIND

Some people regard changing their mind as a sign of weakness and will rigidly stick to a decision as a matter of principle. But circumstances sometimes change so that it becomes prudent to change your mind. It is OK to change your mind when there is a logical reason for doing so. A class rule should be changed, for instance, if the teacher has evidence that it is not working. To be able to be flexible is the mark of the high self-esteem person.

TAKE TIME TO MAKE DECISIONS

We all tend to place a premium on making quick decisions. People are often pushed into doing so and are expected to make a decision on the spot. This is common at staff meetings when teachers do not want to be thought to be 'ditherers'. The fact is that it is not always easy to make a quick decision without some considerable thought. Where this is the case, people should not be afraid to ask for time before responding.

MAKE YOUR NEEDS KNOWN

Assertiveness training has assumed a popularity these days amongst courses on self-development. As there is a positive correlation between assertiveness and self-esteem all teachers need to be sure they are appropriately assertive. This does not mean being aggressive. Indeed, it is possible to rate yourself along a dimension of assertiveness from 'submissive' at one end of a scale to 'aggressive' at the other end. We should aim to be at the midpoint on this scale:

Submissive → Assertive → Aggressive

The submissive teacher would be unable to express controversial opinions at a staff meeting. These teachers tend to avoid unpleasant situations or conflict with others. The aggressive teacher would not be so reticent but would be inclined to express themselves in an unpleasant fashion, demanding others accept their views and demanding their needs be satisfied. Assertive teachers are unafraid to say what they mean or what they want, expressing themselves politely but firmly. They are calm in their presentations and are ready to repeat their needs if necessary.

There is another type of teacher who may not be lacking in assertion so much as lacking the capacity to empathize with others. At a staff meeting, for instance, this kind of teacher would tend to assume that the others at the meeting know him/her well enough to be able to know what he/she wants or what he/she is thinking. The reality can be very different as people often see things in different ways and from different perspectives. This assumption can lead to disappointments and some degree of stress as, after a meeting is over, they realize their views have not been taken into account. We cannot always guarantee that others will automatically know what we want without our saying what it is. So it is important always to state our needs firmly but politely when decisions are being made which affect our welfare or our method of operation.

Teachers might like to assess their self-esteem levels using the following questionnaire.

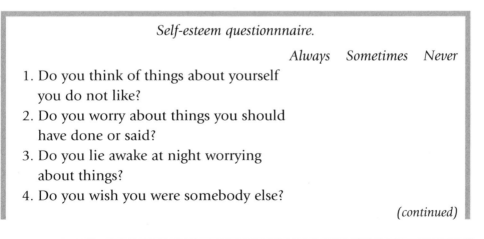

Self-esteem questionnnaire.

	Always	*Sometimes*	*Never*
1. Do you think of things about yourself you do not like?			
2. Do you worry about things you should have done or said?			
3. Do you lie awake at night worrying about things?			
4. Do you wish you were somebody else?			

(continued)

Always   Sometimes   Never

5. Do you hate having to return faulty goods to a shop?
6. Do other people criticize you for what you do or say?
7. Are you easily hurt when people find fault with you?
8. Do you try to avoid difficult meetings?
9. Do you feel that lots of people dislike you?
10. Do you worry about past mistakes?
11. Do you give in easily when faced with difficult tasks?
12. Do you dislike the sound of your voice?
13. Are you ashamed of your background?
14. Are you anxious when having to meet a new person?
15. Are you able to think clearly when in a conversation?
16. Are you easily embarrassed?
17. Would you take a drug to help you get through a meeting?
18. Do you dislike your appearance?
19. Are other people more popular than you?
20. Do you find it hard to make up your mind?

Score: Always = 0 Sometimes = 1 Never = 2
           Scores between 0 and 20 = Low self-esteem
           Scores between 21 and 30 = Average self-esteem
           Scores between 31 and 40 = High self-esteem

■ SELF-ESTEEM AND TEACHER STRESS ■

The relationship between teacher stress and low self-esteem is part of a vicious circle as when teachers suffer from stress their self-esteem drops. This affects children's self-esteem which, in turn, affects their achievements and their behaviour. The circle continues with teachers being put under stress by difficult children, and so it goes on.

Whenever people suffer from stress their self-esteem is immediately put at risk. People feel guilty when they have to admit that they may not be able to cope with the demands of the job. Teaching is no exception to this. In fact, the evidence points very firmly to the view that, of all the professions, teaching is potentially the most stressful. In a large survey conducted by Cox (1978), 70 per cent of teachers mentioned the job itself as their main source of stress. This was compared with only 38 per cent of people in other professions surveyed who considered the job to be their main source of stress. Admittedly this research took place almost 20 years ago but there are firm grounds for believing that today teacher stress is even more common. There is plenty of evidence to show that the very nature of the work done is conducive to stress amongst the most stable of teachers. The irony is that unless people have been teachers they can have little appreciation of this fact. To the outsider it appears to be a very congenial job indeed, with its short hours and long holidays. To those who are teachers or have been teachers this is far from the truth.

Most research today points to job overload, difficult children and feelings of inadequacy as the sources of teacher stress, with feelings of inadequacy more likely to be the end product rather than a main source of stress. In other words, teachers are all at risk of suffering low self-esteem.

Definitions of stress vary but the one by McGrath (1970) is probably the one most easily recognized by teachers: 'a perceived substantial imbalance between demand and response capability, under conditions where failure to meet demand has important perceived consequences'. The consequences for teachers can range from irritability and headaches to the more serious nervous breakdown. From the point of view of teacher self-esteem, clearly, it is important first for teachers to recognize that they are at risk and then for them to learn strategies for preventing it.

All schools should try to arrange regular staff meetings in an informal, non-threatening setting where they would be encouraged to discuss problems faced in the classroom. This is commonly found in industry, sometimes with staff enjoying the luxury of an overnight stay in a first-class hotel. The starting point is first to accept that all teachers will have problems and not to feel it is some kind of character defect to have to admit it. Practical help can be given at these meetings by teachers who have

Four-step method of stress management

Step 1: What you feel Under this heading try to recall the precise feelings. It is essential you are accurate. For example, did you really feel panic or was it merely the milder feeling of apprehension? Once recalled, the feelings should be written down.

Step 2: What you think Write down the precise thoughts which go through your head when having the feelings. This is not always easy and people sometimes say 'I wasn't thinking anything; I was too scared' or whatever. Even if you are one of these people, do persist until you eventually identify the feelings.

Step 3: What you did Write down what you did at the time of the stress, for example, did you cry/run away, complain, and so on?

Step 4: The treatment stage First you should practise a relaxation technique. There are many different methods of relaxation and you should choose the one which works best for you. One popular method is to relax the muscles of the body in turn, beginning first with the toes and gradually working up the body to the head, focusing particularly on the neck and shoulders. Finally, focus on the stomach muscles and the breathing. After every exhale you should say the word 'relax'. This should be done 20 times. Once relaxed you should visualize your stress situation, only this time see it as a positive scene, that is, with no stress. At the same time you should say quietly to yourself a series of positive affirmations, that is, 'I am a confident person – I like myself and others like me – I am now able to cope with this without stress'.

This procedure should be repeated each day until complete relief is obtained.

experienced the same kind of problems. Additionally, the emotional support experienced can be invaluable in combating stress.

The four-step method of stress management, is outlined above. This is a technique which has been described by some as 'self-hypnosis'. It is based on the observations that: (1) relaxation is incompatible with stress, and (2) the word *relax* is associated with feelings of relaxation.

Teachers who wonder whether they may already be suffering from stress should complete the following questionnaire.

Teachers' stress questionnaire

Yes   No   Unsure

1. I worry that I may not be able to meet deadlines.
2. I find that I often get angry with the children.
3. Nobody at work appreciates my efforts.
4. There are members of staff I do not like.
5. There are lots of children who do not like me.
6. More than one person at work dislikes me.
7. People at work often talk behind my back.
8. I wake up in the middle of the night for no reason.
9. I have trouble getting off to sleep easily.
10. I often have headaches or other pains.
11. I suffer from indigestion.
12. I have no time to read a book or a newspaper.
13. I do not take regular exercise.
14. I find I am interrupting people in conversation more than usual.
15. I find I often forget things, for example, books, meetings, instructions.
16. I often feel like crying when discussing emotional events.
17. I am drinking more than I usually do.
18. I find I have to take work home I would normally finish at school.
19. My weight has altered noticeably during this term.
20. I find my facial muscles are tense and sometimes twitch.

Give yourself two points for all questions answering *yes* and one point

(continued)

for all questions answering *unsure*. Sum your score. The higher it is the greater the stress, as follows:

Scores ranging from 30 to 40 = severe stress requiring professional help.
Scores ranging from 20 to 30 = moderate stress: use the four-step method.
Scores ranging from 5 to 20 = mild stress: take appropriate action.
Scores ranging from 0 to 5 = absence of stress.

Teachers might find the following coping strategies checklist helpful for preventing stress.

Self-help for preventing stress
1. Accept the fact that you may have to face stress situations simply because you are a teacher.
2. List possible areas of stress. You cannot cope with stress by denying it.
3. Nurture yourself by taking time out to have fun.
4. Try not to keep company with people known to be miserable and unhappy.
5. Learn to say 'No' when people make too many demands on you.
6. Practise being assertive and making your needs known.
7. Delegate work wherever possible, both at home as well as in teaching.
8. Listen to your body and recognize that your energies are not limitless.
9. Take regular exercise and eat and drink in moderation.
10. Learn relaxation techniques.

■FURTHER READING■

Fontana, D. (1989) *Managing Stress*, London, BPS/Routledge.

Gold, Y. and Roth, R. (1993) *Teachers Managing Stress and Presenting Burnout*, London, Falmer.

Travers, C. and Cooper, C. (1995) *Teachers Under Pressure: Stress in the Teaching Profession*, London, Routledge.

Conclusion

Despite our technological achievements, humankind has still not found the answer to how best to live peaceably. Understanding and accepting differences in other people continues to be a problem, whether of different gender, race or religion. Whilst individuals and governments continue to seek a solution to these challenges, a major resource for a more assured solution resides within our schools. It is increased investment in the education of our children that is most likely in the long run to make a difference, with a stronger emphasis on social education.

The need for self-esteem enhancement programmes in schools is well established by the research. Programmes in the classroom that encourage in the children the growth of the personal qualities of acceptance, genuineness and empathy provide the basis for the future responsible adult. The child with high self-esteem has a greater chance of developing into an adult with high self-esteem and so would be more likely to contribute to the well-being of others in society.

Teachers in the classroom are in a powerful position to be able to make a positive contribution to the development of children's self-esteem and to set them on the road to becoming responsible and caring adults. It is hoped that this book will have encouraged and helped teachers to appreciate their role in this important task.

■ FURTHER READING ■

Argyle, M. (1987) *The Psychology of Happiness*, Oxford, Oxford University Press.

Dryden, W. and Gordon, J. (1994) *Think Your Way To Happiness*, London, Sheldon Press.

Rees, G. (1991) *Assertion Training*, London, Routledge.

Seligman, M. (1991) *Learned Optimism*, London, Random House.

Appendix: Investigations into self-esteem enhancement and reading attainment

■ PROJECT – 1970■

In 1970, four primary schools in Somerset, England, valiantly agreed to participate in a project designed to investigate the possibility of enhancing self-esteem amongst retarded readers. The four schools each submitted lists of children retarded in reading from which 12 children aged 8–9 years were matched on chronological age, sex, reading age and socio-economic group. Each was then subjected to a different treatment.

Group 1 received remedial reading from a remedial specialist. Group 2 received remedial reading plus individual counselling to enhance self-esteem. Group 3 received counselling only, and Group 4 received ordinary class teaching. The experiment ran for 20 weeks, following which it was discovered that the 'counselling only' group (Group 3) had made the most progress not only in self-esteem enhancement, but also in reading. Second came Group 2, 'remedial reading plus counselling'; third was Group 1, 'remedial reading only'; and Group 4 was last, 'ordinary class teaching' (Lawrence, 1971).

This was the first of a series of experiments by me into methods of self-esteem enhancement amongst primary-school children (Lawrence, 1971;

1972a; 1973; 1982; 1983; 1985).

■ PROJECT – 1984 ■

The latest experiment in the series consisted of 372 eight year old children who were retarding in reading, and they were put into four different treatment groups.

DISTAR ONLY – GROUP A

Group A received instruction in the skills of reading through the Direct Instruction in the Teaching of Arithmetic and Reading (DISTAR) technique devised by Engelmann and others (1969), published by Science Research Associates. The teachers using the method were trained for the experiment by a manager of Marketing Services (UK). She visited the teachers on four occasions before the experiment and at regular intervals during the experiment. The teaching was conducted in groups of 6–10 children, the exact number being determined by the numbers identified in each school. They received instruction three times per week for one-hour sessions. The programme continued for 20 weeks.

DISTAR PLUS COUNSELLING – GROUP B

Group B received treatment in exactly the same manner as the children in Group A. In addition they received counselling once a week for 20 weeks by non-professionals. The children were seen in pairs, each session lasting for 45 minutes. The counsellors were selected by the headteachers of the schools involved and numbered 35 altogether, working in eight different schools. They were met four times before the experiment during which they were given 'handouts' on how to structure the sessions with games and activities designed either by the author or those described by Canfield and Wells (1976). They were also briefed on self-concept theory and on the establishment of empathy as described by Rogers (1975) and 'modelling' as described by Bandura (1977). The essence of this treatment was the quality of the relationship which set out to be accepting and non-judgemental. An atmosphere of trust was established within which the children felt free to confide. The counsellors provided a confident, relaxed model. A combination of humanistic and learning theory principles were attempted.

DISTAR PLUS DRAMA – GROUP C

The children in Group C received DISTAR remedial reading as in the two previous groups, but also received a weekly drama session designed to enhance self-esteem. There were six schools involved in this treatment and groups varied in size from 7 to 15. The sessions were taken by the County Adviser for Drama and each lasted for approximately 45 minutes. The sessions were structured to allow the children to 'take risks' and experience success, as well as through role-playing of 'experts', for example, they would be on an imaginary journey and each given a different expert role. Each member had to consult with the appropriate expert before taking action. The rule was that no criticism of the expert was allowed.

ORDINARY CLASS TEACHING – GROUP D

Group D remained in the ordinary class situation receiving help as usual from their classteacher.

Once again statistically significant differences between groups were obtained with the groups receiving the counselling and the drama treatments showing most gains in self-esteem and in reading attainment. The results of this experiment showed a split in the self-esteem scores at the median point, thus analysing low self-esteem and higher self-esteem scores separately (for the full details of this experiment, see Lawrence, 1985).

Bibliography

Allen, P., Begum, J. and Warwick, I. (2004) *You Are Welcome*, London, Sage.

Anthony, G. (1968) Cerebral dominance as an ecological factor in dyslexia, PhD dissertation, New York University.

Argyle, M. (1987) *The Psychology of Happiness*, Oxford, Oxford University Press.

Argyle, M. (1994) The *Psychology of Interpersonal Behaviour*, Harmondsworth, Penguin Books.

Axline, V. (1947) *Play Therapy*, New York, Ballantine Books.

Bandura, A. (1977) *Social Learning Theory*, Englewood Cliffs, NJ, Prentice-Hall.

Barbra, M. and Barbra, A. (1978) *Self-esteem: a classroom affair*, Minneapolis, MN, Winston.

Barker-Lunn, J.C. (1970) *Streaming in the Primary School*, Slough, NFER.

Barry, C., Frick, P. and Killian, A. (2003) The relation of narcissism and self-esteem conduct problems in children. A preliminary investigation, *Journal of Clinical Child and Adolescent Psychology*, Vol. 32, 1, pp. 139–52.

Baughman, J. (1919) *Handbook of Humor in Education*, West Nyack, NY, Parker.

Baumeister, R.F., Smart, L. and Boden, J.M. (1996) Reaction of threatened egotism to violence and aggression: the dark side of high self-esteem,

Psychological Review, pp. 1035–7. Vol. 103 (1), pp. 5–33.

Beker, J. (1960) The influence of school camping on the self-concepts and social relationships of sixth grade school children, *Journal of Educational Psychology*, Vol. 51, pp. 352–6.

Bowlby, J. (1951) *Child Care and the Growth of Love*, Harmondsworth, Penguin.

Branden (1999) *6 Pillars of Self-Esteem*, New York, Bantam Books.

Brophy, J. and Good, T. (1974) *Teacher–Student Relationships: Causes and Consequences*, New York, Holt, Rinehart & Winston.

Brown, E.N. (1990) Children with spelling and writing difficulties: an alternative approach, in P. Pumphrey and C. Elliott (eds) *Children's Difficulties in Reading, Spelling and Writing*, Lewes, Falmer.

Bryant, P. and Bradley, L. (1985) *Children's Reading Problems*, Oxford, Blackwell.

Buchanan, A. and Hudson, B.L. (eds) (2000) *Promoting Children's Emotional Well-Being*, Oxford, Oxford University Press.

Buckingham, D. (2000) *After the Death of Childhood: Growing up in the Age of Electronic Media*, Oxford: Blackwell Priory.

Bullock, A. (ed.) (1975) *A Language of Life*, (Bullock Report) London, HMSO.

Burns, R.B. (1975) Attitudes to self and to three categories of others in a student group, *Educational Studies*, Vol. 1, pp. 181–9.

Burns, R.B. (1979a) The influence of various characteristics of others on social distance registered by a student group, *Irish Journal of Psychology*, Vol. 3, pp. 193–205.

Burns, R.B. (1979b) *The Self-Concept Theory, Measurement, Development and Behaviour*, London and New York, Longman.

Burns, R.B. (1982) *Self-Concept Development and Education*, Sydney, Holt, Rinehart & Winston.

Bushman, B.J. and Baumeister, R.F. (1998) Threatened egotism, narcissism, self-esteem, and direct and displaced aggression: Does self-love or self-hate lead to violence? *Journal of Personality and Social Psychology*, 75, 219–29.

Butler, J.M. and Haigh, G.V. (1954) Changes in the relation between self-concept and ideal concepts consequent on client-centred counselling, in T. Rogers and A. Dymond (eds) *Psychotherapy and Personality Change*, Chicago, IL, University Press.

Byrne, D. (1961) The repression-sensitisation scale: rationale, reliability and validity, *Journal of Personality*, Vol. 29, pp. 334–49.

Canfield, J. and Wells, H. (1976) *100 Ways to Enhance Self-Concept in the Classroom*, Englewood Cliffs, NJ, Prentice-Hall.

Carkhuff, R.R. (1969) *Helping and Human Relations*, Vol. 1, New York, Holt, Rinehart & Winston.

Carkhuff, R.R. and Truax, C.B. (1967) *Towards Effective Counselling and Psychotherapy in Training and Practice*, Chicago, IL, Aldine.

Cashdan, A. and Pumfrey, P. (1969) Some effects of the remedial teaching of reading, *Educational Research*, Vol. 11, no. 7, pp. 138–47.

Chapman, J.W. and Tunmer, W.E. (2003) Reading difficulties, reading related self-perceptions, and strategies for overcoming negative self-beliefs, *Reading and Writing Quarterly*, Vol. 19, pp. 5–24.

Charles, C. (1995) *Building Classroom Discipline*, Harlow, Longman.

Chazan, M. (1967) The effects of remedial teaching in reading: a review of research, *Remedial Education*, Vol. 2, no. 1, pp. 4–12.

Cherniss, C. (1995) *Beyond Burnout: Helping Teachers, Nurses, Therapists and Lawyers Recover from Stress*, London, Routledge.

Clark, J.(1978) *Self-Esteem: A Family Affair*, Minneapolis, MN, Winston.

Collins, J.E. (1961) *The Effects of Remedial Education*, London, Oliver & Boyd.

Collins, M. (2002) *Because I'm Special*, London, Sage.

Combs, A.W., Soper, D.W. and Courson, C.C. (1963) The measurement of self-concept and self-report, *Educational and Psychological Measurement*, Vol. 23, pp. 493–500.

Cooley, C.H. (1902) *Human Nature and the Social Order*, New York, Charles Scribner's Sons.

Coopersmith, S. (1967) *The Antecedents of Self-Esteem*, San Francisco, CA, Freeman Press.

Covington, M. (1989) *Self-esteem and Failure in School: The Social Importance of Self-esteem*, Berkeley, CA, UCA.

Cowie, H. and Pecherek, A. (1994) *Counselling: Approaches and Issues in Education*, London, Fulton.

Cox, T. (1978) *Stress*, Basingstoke, Macmillan.

Crocker, J. and Wolfe, C.T. (2001) Contingencies of self-worth, *Psychological Review*, Vol. 108, pp. 593–623.

Crowley, C., Hallam, S., Harre, R. and Lunt, I. (2001) Study support for young people with same-sex attraction: views and experiences from a pioneering peer support initiative in the north of England, *Educational and Child Psychology*, Vol. 18, no. 1, pp. 108–24.

Davies, G. (1999) *Six Years of Circle Time*, London, Sage.

Davies, J. and Brember, I. (1999) Reading and mathematics attainments and self-esteem in Years 2 and 6 – an eight year cross-sectional study, *Educational Studies*, Vol. 25, pp. 145–57.

De Charms, R. (1976) *Enhancing Motivation in the Classroom*, New York, Irvington.

Department for Education and Skills (DfES) (2003) *Every Child Matters*, London, The Stationery Office.

Department for Education and Skills (DfES) (2004) *Every Child Matters: Next Steps*, London, The Stationery Office.

Dewhurst, D. (1991) Should teachers enhance their pupils' self-esteem? *Journal of Moral Education*, Vol. 20, no. 1, pp. 3–11.

Dryden, W. (1995) *Brief Rational/Emotive Behaviour Therapy*, Chichester, Wiley.

Dryden, W. and Gordon, J. (1994) *Think Your Way to Happiness*, London, Sheldon Press.

Edwards, J. (1994) *The Scars of Dyslexia*, London, Cassell.

Ellis, A. (1979) *Theoretical and Empirical Foundations of Rational and Emotive Therapy*, Monterey, CA, Brooks/Cole.

Elmer, N. (2001) *Self-Esteem: The Costs and Causes of Low Self Worth*, York, Joseph Rowntree Foundation.

Englemann, S., Osborn, E. and Englemann, J. (1969) *DISTAR: An Instructional System*, Language I, II, III; Reading I, II, III; Arithmetic I, II, III, Chicago, IL, SRA.

English, H.B. and English, A.C. (1958) *A Comprehensive Dictionary of Psychological and Psychoanalytical Terms*, London, Longman.

Erickson, E. (1974) *Identity, Youth and Crises*, London, Faber & Faber.

Everhart, R.B. (1985) On feeling good about oneself: practical ideology in schools of choice, *Sociological Education*, Vol. 58, pp. 251–60.

Eysenck, H. (1980) *Psychology Is About People*, Harmondsworth, Penguin.

Farnham, G. and Diggory, S. (1978) *Learning Disabilities*, London, Fontana.

Flowers, J.V. (1991) A behavioural method of increasing self-confidence in elementary school children: treatment and modelling results, *British Journal of Educational Psychology*, Vol. 61, pp. 13–18.

Fontana, D. (1981) *Psychology For Teachers*, London, Macmillan Press.

Fontana, D. (1989) *Managing Stress*, London, British Psychological Society, Routledge.

Galbraith, A. and Alexander, J. (2005) Literacy self-esteem and locus of control, *Support For Learning*, Vol. 20, no. 1, pp. 28–34.

Gammage, P. (1986) *Primary Education: Structure and Context*, London, Paul Chapman Publishing.

Giddens, A. (1991) *Modernity and Self-identity: Self and Society in the Late Modern Age*, Cambridge, Polity.

Gold, Y. and Roth, R. (1993) *Teachers Managing Stress and Presenting Burnout*, London, Falmer.

Gordon, T. (1970) *Parent Effectiveness Training*, New York, Wyden.

Gordon, T. (1972) *Teacher-effectiveness Training*, New York, Wyden.

Gordon, T. (1974) *Teacher Effectiveness Training*, New York, Wyden.

Gray, P., Miller, A. and Nockes, J. (eds) (1994) *Challenging Behaviour In Schools*, London, Routledge.

Greenhalgh, P. (1994) *Emotional Growth and Learning*, London, Routledge.

Haigh, G. (1994) *Managing Classroom Problems in the Primary School*, London, Paul Chapman Publishing.

Hanko, G. (1985) *Special Needs in Ordinary Classrooms: Supporting Teachers*, Oxford, Blackwell.

Hannum, J.W. (1974) Changing the evaluative self thoughts of two elementary teachers, *Research and Development Memorandum No. 122*, Stanford University, CA.

Hargie, R., Saunders, J. and Dickson, L. (1995) *Social Skills in Interpersonal Communication*, London, Routledge.

Hargreaves, D. (1972) *Interpersonal Relations and Education*, London, Routledge.

Harris, T. (1969) *I'm OK – You're OK*, London, Pan Books.

James, W. (1890) *Principles of Psychology*, Vol. 1, New York, Henry Holt.

Jenks C. (1996) *Childhood*, London, Routledge.

Jung, C. (1923) *Psychological Types*, New York, Harcourt Brace.

Katz, L. (1993) Distinction between self-esteem and narcissism: implications for practice, Eric/EECE, Archive of Publications and Resources, University of Illinois.

Lau, A. (ed.) (2000) *South Asian Children and Adolescents in Britain*, London, Whurr.

Lawrence, A. (2004) *Principles of Child Protection: Management and Practice*, Maidenhead, McGraw-Hill.

Lawrence, A. and Lawrence, D. (1996) *Self-Esteem and Your Child*, London, Minerva Press.

Lawrence, D. (1971) The effects of counselling on retarded readers, *Educational Research*, Vol. 13, no. 2, pp. 119–24.

Lawrence, D. (1972a) An experimental investigation into the counselling of retarded readers, unpublished MSc dissertation, University of Bristol.

Lawrence, D. (1972b) Counselling of retarded readers by non-professionals, *Educational Research*, Vol. 15, no. 1, pp. 48–54.

Lawrence, D. (1973) *Improved Reading through Counselling*, London, Ward Lock.

Lawrence, D. (1982) Development of a self-esteem questionnaire, *British Journal of Educational Psychology*, Vol. 51, pp. 245–9.

Lawrence, D. (1983) Improving reading and self-esteem, unpublished PhD thesis, University of Western Australia.

Lawrence, D. (1985) Improving reading and self-esteem, *Educational Research*, Vol. 27, no. 3, pp. 194–200.

Lawrence, D. (1999) *Teaching with Confidence: A Guide to Enhancing Teacher Self-Esteem*, London, Paul Chapman Publishing.

Lawrence, D. and Blagg, N. (1974) Improved reading through self-initiated learning and counselling, *Remedial Education*, Vol. 9, no. 2, pp. 61–3.

Lowen, A. (2004) *Narcissism: Denial of the True Self*, New York, Simon & Schuster.

Lunn, J.C.B. (1970) *Streaming in the Primary School*, Slough, NFER.

Machover, K. (1949) *Personality Projection in the Drawing of the Human Figure: A Method of Personality Investigation*, Springfield, IL, Charles C. Thomas.

MacKay, T. and Watson, K. (1999) Literacy social disadvantage and early intervention: enhancing reading achievement in primary schools, *Educational and Child Psychology*, Vol. 16, no. 1, pp. 30–36.

Maines, B. (2003) *Reading Faces*, London, Sage.

Maines, B. and Robinson, G. (1990) *B/G Scale*, Bristol, Lucky Duck.

Marsh, H.W., Barnes, J., Cairns, L. and Tidman, M. (1984) The self-description questionnaire: age effects in the structure and level of self-concept for pre-adolescent children, *Journal of Educational Psychology*, Vol. 76, pp. 940–56.

Marston, A.R. (1986) Dealing with low self-confidence, *Educational Research*, Vol. 10, pp. 134–8.

Maslow, A.H. (1954) *Motivation and Personality*, 2nd edn, New York, Harper & Row.

Maslow, A.H. (1962) Some basic propositions of a growth and self-actualization psychology, in A.W. Combs (ed.) *Perceiving, Behaving, Becoming*, ASCD Year Book, Washington, DC, NEA.

McGrath, J.E. (1970) *Social and Psychological Factors in Stress*, New York, Holt, Reinhart and Winston.

Merrett, F. and Wheldall, K. (1990) *Positive Teaching in the Primary School*, London, Paul Chapman Publishing.

Miles, T. and Haslum, M.N. (1986) Dyslexia: anomaly and normal variation? *Annals of Dyslexia*, 36, pp. 103–17.

Miles, T. and Miles, E. (1999) *Dyslexia: One Hundred Years On*, (2nd ed.) Milton Keynes, Open University Press.

Morris, E. and Morris, K. (1999) *The Powerhouse*, Bristol, Lucky Duck.

Mrak, C.J. (1999) *Self-Esteem, Research, Theory and Practice (1999)*, 2nd ed. New York, Springer. pp. 141–56.

Murray, E. (1972) Students' perceptions of self-actualising and non self-actualising teachers, *Journal of Teacher Education*, Vol. 23, pp. 383–7.

Neill, R. (1991) *Classroom Non-verbal Communication*, London, Routledge.

Omwake, K. (1954) The relation between acceptance of self and acceptance of others shown by three personality inventories, *Journal of Consulting Psychology*, Vol. 18, no. 6, pp. 443–6.

Osgood, C., Suci, G. and Tannenbaum, P. (1957) *The Measurement of*

Meaning, Urbana, IL, University of Illinois Press.

Perkins, H.V. (1958) Teacher's and peers' perception of children's self-concepts, *Child Development*, Vol. 29, no. 2, pp. 203–20.

Piers, E.V. and Harris, D. (1969) *The Piers–Harris Children's Self-Concept Scale*, Nashville, TN, Counsellor Recordings and Tests,

Pratt, J. (1978) Perceived stress among teachers, *Educational Review*, Vol. 30, no. 1, pp. 3–14.

Priestly, P. and McGuire, J. (1986) *Learning to Help: Basic Skills Exercises*, London, Tavistock.

Pumphrey, P.D. and Reason, R. (1991) *Specific Learning Difficulties (Dyslexia), Challenges and Responses*, Windsor, NFER-Nelson.

Purkey, W. (1970) *Self-concept and School Achievement*, Englewood Cliffs, NJ, Prentice-Hall.

Rae, T. (1999) *Confidence, Assertiveness, Self-esteem*, Bristol, Lucky Duck.

Rae, T. (2000) *Confidence, Assertiveness, Self-esteem*, London, Sage.

Rees, G. (1991) *Assertion Training*, London, Routledge.

Roberts, R. (2002) *Self-esteem and Early Learning*, 2nd edn, London, Paul Chapman Publishing.

Robinson, G. and Maines, B. (1992) *No Blame Approach*, London, Sage.

Robinson, G. and Maines, B. (1997) *Crying For Help: The No Blame Approach to Bullying*, Bristol, Lucky Duck.

Roffey, S., Tarrant, T. and Majors, K. (1994) *Young Friends: Schools and Friendships*, London, Cassell.

Rogers, C.R. (1951) *Client-centered Therapy*, Boston, MA, Houghton Mifflin.

Rogers, C.R. (1961) *On Becoming a Person*, Boston, MA, Houghton Mifflin.

Rogers, C.R. (1967) *On Becoming a Person*, London, Constable.

Rogers, C.R. (1969) *Freedom to Learn. A View of What Education Might Become*, Columbus, OH, Merrill.

Rogers, C.R. (1970) *Encounter Groups*, New York, Harper & Rowe.

Rogers, C.R. (1975) Empathy: an unappreciated way of being, *The Counselling Psychologist*, Vol. 5, no. 2, pp. 2–9.

Rosenberg, M. (1965) *Society and the Adolescent and Self-Image*, Princeton University Press.

Rosenberg, M., Schooler, C., Schoenbach, R. and Rosenberg, F. (1995) Global self-esteem, specific self-esteem: different concepts, different outcomes, *American Sociological Review*, Vol. 60, February, pp. 141–56.

Rosenthal, R. and Jacobson, L. (1968) Self-fulfilling prophecies in the classroom: teacher expectations as unintended determinants of pupils' intellectual competence, in M. Deutsch, I. Katz and A.C. Jenson (eds) *Social Class, Race and Psychological Development*, New York, Holt, Rinehart & Winston.

Rotter, J.B. (1954) *Social Learning and Clinical Psychology*, Englewood Cliffs, NJ, Prentice-Hall.

Rutter, M., Maughan, B., Mortimore, R. and Ouston, J. (1979) *Fifteen Thousand Hours: Secondary Schools and their Effects on Children*, London, Paul Chapman Publishing.

Schweinhart, L.J., Weikart, D.R. and Larner, M.B. (1986) Consequences of three pre-school curriculum models, *Early Childhood Research Quarterly*, Vol. 1, no. 1, pp. 15–45.

Sedikides, C. and Kumashiro, M. (2005) On the resource function of relationships. Close positive relationships as a dissonance reduction mechanism, unpublished manuscript, University of Southampton.

Seligman, M. (1991) *Learned Optimism*, London, Random House.

Sharp, G. and Muller, D. (1978) The effects of lowering self-concept on associative learning, *Journal of Psychology*, Vol. 100, pp. 233–42.

Shavelson, R.J. and Bolus, R. (1982) Self-concept: the interplay of theory and methods, *Journal of Educational Psychology*, Vol. 74, no. 1, pp. 3–17.

Shavelson, R.J., Hubner, J.J. and Stanton, G.G. (1976) Self-concept: validation of construct interpretations, *Review of Education Research*, Vol. 46, pp. 407–41.

Skinner, B.F. (1953) *Science and Human Behavior*, New York, Macmillan.

Smith, C.E (ed.) (1969) *Achievement Related Motives in Children*, New York, Russell Sage Foundation.

Snowling, M.J. (1995) Phonological processing and developmental dyslexia, *Journal of Research In Reading*, Vol. 18, pp. 132–8.

Staines, J.W. (1958) Self picture as a factor in the classroom, *British Journal of Psychology*, Vol. 28, no. 2, pp. 97–111.

Stalman, D. (1993) Self-assessment, self-esteem, and self-acceptance, *Journal of Moral Education*, Vol. 22, no. 1.

Stevens, R. (ed.) (1995) *Understanding the Self*, Sage, London.

Stott, D. (1966) *Troublesome Children*, London, Tavistock Publications.

Thomas, J.B. (1973) *Self-Concept in Psychology and Education*, Slough, NFER.

Thomas, J.B. (1980) *The Self in Education*, Slough, NFER.

Travers, C. and Cooper, C. (1995) *Teachers Under Pressure: Stress in the Teaching Profession*, London, Routledge.

Trowbridge, N. (1973) Teacher self-concept and teaching style, in G. Chanan (ed.) *Towards a Science of Teaching*, Slough, NFER.

Troyna, B. and Hatcher, R. (1992) *Racism in Children's Lives: A Study of Mainly White Primary Schools*, London, Routledge.

Warwick, I., Oliver, C. and Aggleton, P. (2000) Sexuality and mental health promotion: lesbian and gay young people, in P. Aggleton, J. Hurry and I. Warwick (eds) *Young People and Mental Health*, Chichester, Wiley.

Wattenburg, W.W. and Clifford, C. (1964) Relation of self-concept to beginning achievement in reading, *Child Development*, Vol. 35, pp. 461–7.

Wells, L. and Marwell, G. (1982) *Self-esteem: Its Conceptualisation and Its Measurement*, London, Sage Publications.

West, C.R., Fish, J.A. and Stevens, J.A. (1980) General self-concept, self-concept of academic ability and school achievement, *Australian Journal of Education*, Vol. 24, pp. 194–213.

White, M. (1999) *Magic Circles*, London, Sage.

Wiseman, S. (1973) The educational obstacle race: factors that hinder pupil progress, *Education Research*, Vol. 15, pp. 87–93.

Woolfe, R. and Dryden, W. (eds) (1996) *Handbook of Counselling Psychology*, London, Sage.

Wravers, C.J. and Cooper, C.L. (1995) *Teachers under Pressure: Stress in the Teaching Profession*, London, Routledge.

Wylie, R. (1974) *The Self-Concept*, 2nd edn, Lincoln, NE, University of Nebraska Press.

Young, L. and Bagley, C. (1982) Self esteem, self concept and the development of black identity: a theoretical overview, in G. Verma, and C. Bagley (eds) *Self Concept Achievement and Multicultural Education*, London, Macmillan.

Yule, W. and Gold, A. (1993) *Wise Before the Event: Coping with Crises in Schools*, London, Calouste Gulbenkian Foundation.

Index